Implementing Word of Mouth Marketing

Implementing Word of Mouth Marketing

Online Strategies to Identify Influencers, Craft Stories, and Draw Customers

Idil Miriam Cakim

WILEY

John Wiley & Sons, Inc.

Published by John Wiley & Sons, Inc., Hoboken, New Jersey.
Published simultaneously in Canada.

For general information on our other products and services or for technical support, please contact our Customer Care Department within the United States at (800) 762-2974, outside the United States at (317) 572-3993 or fax (317) 572-4002.

Wiley also publishes its books in a variety of electronic formats. Some content that appears in print may not be available in electronic books. For more information about Wiley products, visit our web site at www.wiley.com.

Library of Congress Cataloging-in-Publication Data:
Cakim, Idil M., 1974–
    Implementing word of mouth marketing : online strategies to identify influencers, craft stories, and draw customers / Idil M. Cakim.
      p. cm.
    Includes index.
    ISBN 978-0-470-44255-5 (hardback)
     1. Word-of-mouth advertising. 2. Telemarketing. I. Title.
    HF5827.95.C35 2010
    658.8'72—dc22   2009029115

Printed in the United States of America
10 9 8 7 6 5 4 3 2 1

To my family

Contents

Contents

Contents

Contents

Contents

Preface

Why the Internet Matters More Now

In the heyday of the dot-com era, I was working at a promising small company on Hudson Street in New York City, where many Internet start-ups had offices. We researched Internet-related trends and published industry briefs, telling brick-and-mortar companies to bring their businesses online and finding new audiences for online companies. AOL was becoming mainstream. The number of Internet users was multiplying every quarter. Business was pouring in. We were growing at an incredible speed, interviewing new candidates almost every day. We were on the cutting edge. We were the future.

Then came the dot-com bust. In March 2000, the market went on a steep decline. Many dot-coms ceased to exist. Many more had to lay off their staff. I remember walking on Hudson and seeing people with hunched shoulders, carrying their personal belongings from their offices back to their homes. One tearful young woman was sobbing: "But I worked so, so hard. I worked so hard." She had just lost her job. All that hope for success and innovation seemed to have evaporated in a flash.

The market crash did not diminish the power of the Internet. People continued to rely on the Web for information, connectivity, and entertainment. New businesses emerged to fulfill the demand. At times, they created demand. Nowadays, organizations are far from debating the validity of investing in online channels. It is no longer a question of *if*, but *how*.

I wrote this book during one of the biggest financial crises the United States has seen in decades. Every time I read about jobless claims, I think back to that time on Hudson Street. There is hope.

While we may have lesser means, we are also part of an extensive and visible network, thanks to the Internet and social media platforms. Information flows from one hub to another in a matter of clicks. We are learning to share knowledge and pool our resources. We can reach hundreds with one message posted online, seek guidance, and get useful advice from people we have yet to meet face-to-face.

Today, blogs and social networks are popular. Tomorrow, people will rush to more advanced online platforms. The tools may change but the mode of communication will remain open. Those who understand the advantages of sharing resources will recruit fans and build sizable communities. Smart organizations will tap into online conversations and offer products and services to improve people's lives. These establishments will grow and attain their goals, as they use the Web to earn people's trust and support.

Why I Wrote This Book

I wanted to write a book that showed readers how to create meaningful content and distribute messages effectively through social media channels. In the increasingly crowded Internet space, publishing a blog or launching a page on a social network is no longer sufficient to reach audiences. Content needs to be social, to be connected to a wide web of information, and to show up on search engines to reach far and be visible.

It is unlikely that a video posted on YouTube will become an overnight sensation just because it is listed on a Web page. Most blogs will not garner more than a handful of random followers. Posting content online may be the first step in generating word of mouth online and offline, but there are many additional steps content owners need to take to generate excitement around their news and sustain that momentum over time.

Turning a blog entry into a viral phenomenon may seem like an arduous task. However, organizations can build presence in social media by mimicking public opinion leaders who spark and lead online discussions.

Online influencers hunt for information, share stories, dive into online conversations, engage their audiences, and know many people across a wide range of networks. People seek their opinions and follow their advice.

Organizations can act the same way. Indeed, there is a method to joining online conversations, building online networks, and writing stories that resonate with online audiences.

How This Book Will Help You

Implementing Word of Mouth Marketing is a comprehensive guide to designing online marketing programs that generate authentic and positive conversations. This book provides a strategic framework and practical tips to prepare, launch, and sustain online word of mouth marketing programs. Through current case studies, best practices, and actionable advice, it delivers smart social media plans and cost-effective tactics you can deploy immediately.

The book lists the fundamentals of identifying online influencers, developing messages that draw attention, and choosing the Web-based tools that can drive conversations—online and offline.

It elaborates on these points with a variety of examples from large companies such as PepsiCo and the Ford Motor Company, creative organizations such as Veer and Smarthome, and nonprofits such as Greenpeace International. The book also draws communication lessons from grassroots initiatives that started on Hoboken411 and TOMS Shoe Fans Web sites, among others.

What You Will Find in This Book

Implementing Word of Mouth Marketing spells out the critical advantage of having Internet access in an information-driven society.

Part I makes the claim that those who know how to use the Web to find, gather, and spread information will not only survive, but will thrive.

Part II provides readers with an approach to determine what online influence means to their brands. It offers numerous ways to spot online conversation leaders, earn these influencers' trust, and start long-term relations with them.

Part III addresses the biggest challenges marketers face when launching word of mouth programs. It emphasizes the need to observe social and cultural trends when constructing messages. It shows how to add value to online influencers' conversations. This section explains that successful online initiatives that yield high volumes of word of mouth involve an ongoing dialogue between organizations and their audiences. It points to the direct relationship between quality products and positive word of mouth. It shows how keeping promises to online influencers builds trust and transforms these cybercitizens into advocates.

Part IV demonstrates how to build online word of mouth campaigns that compel influencers to pass along messages. It provides readers with a detailed framework to define success at the planning stages of online initiatives, set benchmarks, and measure the impact of word of mouth during and after communication programs.

The Appendix consists of a list of questions readers can answer as they prepare to design and launch online word of mouth marketing programs. This self-assessment tool will guide practitioners as they conduct their research, articulate their messages, and brainstorm about creative ways to engage their audiences.

Ultimately, the best way to learn about social media and understand how participatory communication channels work is to join the community and blogging platforms mentioned in this book. User names and passwords can help unveil the counterintuitive dynamics of social media and connect you with new, relevant, and powerful audiences. To implement online word of mouth strategies, listen to what they have to say, respond, and stay in touch.

IDIL MIRIAM CAKIM
Brooklyn, New York
December 2009

Acknowledgments

Taking a bold step does not only require courage, but it also takes encouragement. I wrote this book with the support of my family, friends, and colleagues. I am immensely grateful and want to thank you all.

My parents Liza and Yomtov and my brother Can—I cannot thank you enough for all that you have given me. Your love defies borders and traverses continents. Greg, I am blessed to have you in my life, by my side. Thank you for gracing this project with your beautiful drawings.

I would like to extend my gratitude to Ronald Kessler, who said I could write and that I should write. You opened a new door for me. I am forever indebted. Thank you, Pam and Rachel, for all your ideas and fine wordsmithing.

I would not have been talking about online influencers if it were not for that fateful day when I interviewed with Dr. Leslie Gaines-Ross. Leslie, thank you for all that you taught me. Thank you for being my guardian.

I also want to acknowledge my first mentor, Peter Clemente, for his contributions to my career. As an innovator, creator, and author, he has always been a source of inspiration for me.

I owe many thanks to my editors Tim Burgard and Stacey Rivera at Wiley, who believed in my ideas and poured their thoughts into every word I wrote.

Last, but not least, I want to thank my colleagues who cheered me on from day one and presented me with many opportunities to do what I love to do.

Implementing
Word of Mouth
Marketing

PART

I

UNDERSTANDING ONLINE WORD OF MOUTH

The Internet has transformed the way information flows across social circles. Opinion leaders, who can use Web-enabled devices to gather, distribute, and publish information, have the power to lead crowds.

They can reach hundreds of people with a few keystrokes and clicks. Their blogs and social network profiles are knowledge hubs. Their words are news. These networking agents know how to use the Web to their advantage.

CHAPTER 1

The Need for Word of Mouth Information

Anyone living in the information society is exposed to an overwhelming number of marketing messages each day. The noise from branding bombardments mounts to new heights as consumers seek news or entertainment across hundreds of cable TV channels, radio stations, magazines, and newspapers. The sales pitches on television, radio, and in print advertisements are coupled with online advertisements, postings, and chatter.

The 24/7 Web mimics offline media with news and entertainment offerings, while pushing personal messages to consumers' homes and offices. The second consumers turn to search engines and click "Go!" they see lists of links along with advertisements paid by companies that want to be matched with certain key words. Dynamic and flashy content on Web destinations add to visitors' information pile. E-mail messages from companies and organizations fill up in-boxes and wait for their readers.

To manage message overload, consumers sift and drain information. They ignore messages that are out of context or immaterial. They seek products and services from trusted companies. They do their own research and they check up on the facts with people who are in the know. Before making a decision, consumers ask their peers' opinions and rely on the advice of authoritative, experienced people who have had firsthand experience with the product, service, or issue.

Trust in Media

The public relations firm GolinHarris conducted a study asking consumers, ages 18 and older, the degree to which they use, rely upon, and trust various information sources, such as their own direct experience, word of mouth, and traditional and online media. Consumers indicated the information sources they trust today and what they envision themselves trusting in the future. The results culminate in the Trusted Media Index (TMI).

The study points to the significant role word of mouth plays in the mix of information sources consumers rely on and trust as they make everyday decisions. Among the resources consumers trust, traditional media channels such as TV, radio, newspapers, and magazines trail behind word of mouth.

As seen in Exhibit 1.1, word of mouth, direct experience, and online media have the lead among the most trusted sources. Meanwhile, traditional outlets such as television, newspapers, magazines, and radio are trusted less than the information sources that give audiences the opportunity to test, probe, and verify. Today's consumers are cynical about overt marketing

Exhibit 1.1 Information Sources Consumers Trust

Information Sources	Trusted Media Index Score (Average of Today and Future)
Word of mouth	59
Experiential	58
Dedicated online media	58
Radio	56
Television	56
Newspapers	56
Magazines	53
Consumer-generated media	52

Source: Trusted Media Index Study, GolinHarris, 2008.

efforts. After dealing with institutions that fail to deliver on their promises, they do not readily believe professionally crafted messages or the messengers. Instead, they prefer to listen to candid reports from others and do their own research online and offline.

The Rise of Social Media

The study distinguishes between two types of online content. It refers to dedicated online media as all Web-based properties that exist only on the Internet, without support from brick-and-mortar parent companies. The Web portal AOL, the online news and culture site Salon.com, and the health-care information site WebMD.com are examples of dedicated online media. Meanwhile, consumer-generated media refers to blogs, discussion board postings, and social network pages cybercitizens create.

When looking at the average of what consumers trust today and will trust in the future, consumer-generated media does not appear to be among the top choices for the general U.S. consumer population. However, when looking at the difference between today and the perceived future (see Exhibit 1.2), consumer-generated media picks up the most steam among sources the public indicates that they will trust.

Exhibit 1.2 Consumer Trust in Media: Today and in the Future

Information Sources	TMI Score (Today)	TMI Score (Future)	TMI Score (Variance)
Word of mouth	61	57	−3.8
Experiential	58	59	0.4
Dedicated online media	56	60	4.2
Radio	58	54	−3.6
Television	58	54	−3.8
Newspapers	58	53	−4.2
Magazines	53	52	−0.5
Consumer-generated media	48	56	7.9

The rise of trust in consumer-generated media, otherwise known as social media, in the future underscores the changes taking place in the communication landscape. Consumers will become increasingly willing to trust online posts and add them to the mix of information they gather before they make decisions to buy, vote, or join a group. Therefore, companies and organizations that invest in social media today, by building an online presence and connecting with consumers who publish online, will surge ahead of their competitors. They will earn consumers' trust and be part of their conversations, online and offline, as audiences will rely on social media more to get their news.

Online Word of Mouth

The information age has paved the way to the experience economy. Consumers either try products and services firsthand or seek recommendations from others who have already done so. Since it may not be feasible or economical for consumers to test all that they hear about brands in the media, they often rely on others' reports. They talk to their neighbors, e-mail colleagues, and read online customer reviews. In the absence of direct experience, word of mouth has become one of the most valuable sources of information about brands, products, and services.

To harness the power of word of mouth, organizations need to be part of consumer conversations. They need to be prepared for a future where differences between online and face-to-face conversations dissolve and consumers rely on Web-based information sources with as much ease and trust as they do offline sources. To be a leader in today's chaotic communication landscape and to be ready for the future, organizations need to identify and understand those who use the Web effectively to spread their opinions, make their own news, and shake up established institutions.

CHAPTER 2

The Web Advantage

Knowledge of the best available resources has always been a source of competition. People need information to survive and improve their lives. Staying safe, finding food, raising a family, and leading a peaceful life remain our quintessential needs. In fact, we are in constant search of new information that will tell us how to make more money, find better housing, live a life of higher quality, and stay healthy.

We need to compete with others to gain access to limited and diminishing resources. As a result, any morsel of knowledge that can provide an advantage in the race to survive and live well becomes highly desirable. In the experience economy, knowledge is wealth.

The Internet, with its astounding mass of information available to the 1 billion[1] people who use it, tilts the balance of power in the experience economy toward the tech-savvy. The Web empowers proactive consumers who can navigate through pages of online information to uncover critical bits of information.

The advent of open-source Web technologies, which allow Internet users to publish uncensored information online, has added a new level of richness to public information. Thanks to platforms such as online news Web sites, blogs, social networks, and discussion boards, online consumers disseminate

7

critical information about their shopping experiences to other consumers. These tools turn motivated speakers into public opinion leaders who can distribute their ideas to thousands of people with a computer and an Internet connection. The savvy and outspoken Internet users search, navigate, discuss, and publish online, creating relevant and customized information. They act as self-appointed journalists, consumer watchdogs, and spokespeople. They generate and spread information in nano-seconds. The Web enables everyday citizens to spread influence across communities and to become word of mouth agents.

Web-empowered word of mouth agents go beyond their physical neighborhoods and gain significant visibility by posting to message boards and reaching thousands of people. Their computers are communication vehicles that can help or hurt an organization's or an individual's reputation. They can reach hundreds of contacts with one-line updates and can broadcast personal, social, and political messages to widespread communities.

Those who use the Internet with such success are known as networking agents. In the information-saturated society, networking agents are insightful interpreters, uncovering, translating, and spreading critical information. In the new communication order, the networking agents are the knowledge elite. Networking agents can be a member of a variety of demographic or cultural groups—women, men, young, old, middle or high income. Their expertise also varies across topics and industries. Yet, they share a fundamental trait. They have a passion for speaking up and they feel obligated to state their opinion in the name of what they believe is a good cause. They enjoy the participatory nature of a good debate. Networking agents are outspoken people who are committed to research, with access to the latest online communication technologies.

The agents have widespread and diverse networks. When they have something to say, they do not shy from rallying the troops in their local community, writing to the media, or providing feedback to companies. They take it upon themselves to tell their friends and family what to do or give them tips.

Networking agents are information brokers. They gather data and ideas from both online and offline sources. Using search engines, browsing through Web sites, and posting to blogs and message boards, networking agents uncover, forward, talk, and publish information. They can tell a story in person or over the phone. They augment their voices with the help of group e-mails, blogs, and message boards that reach hundreds, if not thousands, of people at a time.

Networking agents can be classified as lean-forward types of audience members who like to create their own news agenda. Their friends, family, and colleagues trust these self-appointed reporters' opinions. As reliable sources, their suggestions turn into purchases, votes, and product trials. To sustain their expert position, networking agents seek information from a variety of sources they deem credible and insightful. They follow the news closely, reading newspapers, watching TV, and scouring the Web for updates. They subscribe to magazines and e-newsletters. They chat online, keeping in touch with colleagues and friends. Rather than feeling overwhelmed with information, they collect, organize, and distribute stories. Online and offline, they are not shy about starting debates. Their use of Web tools to digest information, spread knowledge, and galvanize news deems them uber-information dealers.

To many who are used to receiving their news through the media, these online influencers, called networking agents, are a mystery. Corporate executives, journalists, marketers, activists, and nonprofit leaders who strategize, write, and send approved copy to publishers may have to take a second seat to these ordinary citizens. These citizens can throw a political candidate's prospects into turmoil or shake up established institutions with a paragraph posted to their blogs.

The Power Line

When CBS's *60 Minutes* newscaster Dan Rather claimed that President George W. Bush had used influence to evade the draft and join the Texas Air National Guard, numerous blog authors picked up the story and started an online controversy and debate. Among them, PowerlineBlog.com asserted that the fonts and proportional spacing used in the documents cited by CBS as evidence did not exist in the early 1970s, when President Bush was serving in the National Guard.[2]

Powerline's posting may have evaporated into virtual space, remaining a shout in the dark, had it not been for the high-profile blogger Matt Drudge of the Drudge Report. He took notice and linked to it from his Web site. Once the Drudge Report, which attracts millions of unique visitors a month,[3] covered the forgery claims, rival sources from traditional media took notice and the debate heated up. In the end, CBS formally apologized and admitted that it had compromised journalistic standards by using unverified documents to report a news story. Several CBS executives resigned, Dan Rather's producer was fired, and the veteran journalist ended his respectable career as a CBS news anchor on a sour note.

The Dell Turnaround

The computer maker Dell's ordeal with networking agents did not have to make it to front-page news to tarnish the company's reputation. In 2005, surveys and consumer reports showed that Dell's customer satisfaction scores had been declining. However, it took journalist and professor Jeff Jarvis to publish a heated post on his blog, Buzzmachine, about his frustrating experience with Dell customer service for the issue to be publicized:

> I just got a new Dell laptop and paid a fortune for the four-year, in-home service. The machine is a lemon and the service is a lie. But what really irks me is that they say if they sent someone to my home . . . he wouldn't have the parts . . . [4]

Jarvis got more than 250 comments in response to this blog post. He continued to write about his experience and gathered frustrated Dell customers around him. He coined the term "Dell Hell."

Dell approached networking agent Jarvis and those dissatisfied customers surrounding him with a remarkable and sustainable strategy, rooted in online customer relationship management. The company launched two new communication channels to listen to its customers and speak directly with them. Through the Direct2Dell blog and the IdeaStorm online community, Dell customers and other consumers can now hear Dell news firsthand, reach out to the manufacturer with their comments and questions, and submit new product ideas, telling Dell what they expect from their computers.

Jarvis, a powerful blogger and public figure, lit a fire under the Dell brand. His sentiments resonated with many who struggled with their computers. More important, the Fortune 100 company adopted the ways of networking agents and restored its reputation by opening itself to criticisms and suggestions.

Thoughts on AOL

Not all networking agents are seasoned journalists and academics with connections to business and media. Yet their words can be just as powerful, if their stories resonate with others with similar experiences. When Vincent Ferrari decided to cancel his dormant AOL account, registered under his father's name, he thought a quick phone call to the company's customer service line would resolve the matter. What he faced was an excruciatingly long tug of war with the customer service representative who probed every which way to find reasons why Ferrari wished to cancel the service. The representative tried hard to dissuade him from closing the account.

While AOL had every right to try to keep Ferrari's business, the customer felt frustrated by the experience and found the conversation remarkably pointless. To him, canceling his father's AOL account was a transaction. The tech-savvy Ferrari recorded his conversation with the customer service representative and posted it to his blog, telling his readers how aggravated he was. To date, Ferrari's post has close to 1,000 comments.[5] Since June 2006, when the incident occurred, Internet users who had trouble with technology companies or customer service hotlines have been coming to Ferrari's blog, ironically called Insignificant Thoughts, to vent about their experiences. Some sympathize with the AOL service represent-ative, indicating he was just doing his job, while others concur with Ferrari's sentiments.

Ferrari's blog entry got so much traffic and so many cita-tions on other social media news Web sites that the ruckus caught the attention of the media. The story catapulted into articles on the *New York Times*, CNet News, and MSNBC Web sites, as well as a story on NBC's coveted *Today Show*. Meanwhile, AOL officials reached out to Ferrari and apolo-gized to him, demonstrating their sincerity and professional-ism. Ferrari acknowledged their apology and accepted it in his June 20, 2006, blog entry.[6] Yet the conversation stemming from Ferrari's account of events continues to live online with references dated as recent as 2009.[7]

Networking agents do not have to be journalists or high-ranking bloggers. In contrast to Ferrari, they do not always have to aim at large companies to create impact. Everyday citizens, who have something to share, can create an agenda, build a network, and shake systems up with the help of online tools that facilitate conversation.

Hoboken Online

Hoboken411.com started out as a Web site that introduced visitors to Hoboken through pictures and basic information about the quaint New Jersey town. The Web site's Webmaster put considerable effort into keeping up the Web site and grow-ing it with new content. Over time, Hoboken411.com became a provider of local and political news. Eric Kurta, a gradu-ate student pursuing a degree in political science and public finance, became a frequent reader of the site. In the absence of a dedicated source of local news, Eric found the Web site to be a good way to share information about Hoboken. Many residents, including Eric, submitted information to the Webmaster, who then posted it on the Web site. In addition, visitors who registered with the site could comment on posted articles under their user names. The Web site was a highly valuable source of information to Eric, who had a special interest in local government and budgeting issues. He could connect with people who had been living in Hoboken for more than a decade, as well as those who had just moved to the area, and share his concerns and interests with them.

In 2008, Eric submitted a story to Hoboken411.com about three buildings that were classified as moderate-income housing. In his article, Eric noted that it was not clear why the owner of these buildings was providing housing to people with questionably high incomes and other real estate properties. Through Hoboken411.com, Eric opened a public debate about whether these tenants should be able to stay in the moderate-income buildings or be forced to move out.

Eric's posting on Hoboken411.com spurred a flurry of comments and e-mails among concerned town residents. After communicating through the Web site, some got together in person to strategize and to bring the matter to the attention of city authorities. Volunteers spoke about the issue at Hoboken City Council meetings. The media picked up the story and televised it on the local public access channel. Meanwhile, concerned Hoboken residents flocked to Hoboken411.com. Following this civic activity, the Hoboken City Council asked one of its subcommittees to investigate the matter.

Hoboken411.com connected individuals who had local information but did not necessarily know each other in the offline world. The Web site and vigilant networking agents helped grow the housing story into a public debate about affordable housing. As Eric Kurta pointed out in an interview, Hoboken411.com elevated public activism to new levels by circulating hard-to-find information among a wide network of people. Kurta said,

> For me, part one of the equation is research. Once you have the story, how do you share it, how do you get it out to the community? In the past, you were limited. You could have written a letter to the editor. However, few people read those. Years ago, various groups have come and gone and they've looked at various issues around town. They've handed out flyers and mailed out newsletters. However, that takes a lot of time and considerable amount of money. It just wasn't an efficient way of getting the word out. For someone like me, I'm so grateful, when I come up with an issue, I can type it up, I can send it to the webmaster and he will put it up. [Hoboken411] just changed the way information disseminates.

Transportation Security Administration (TSA) Hears the Laughing Squid

Being present in the blogosphere and listening to online audiences vigilantly will help organizations attend to networking agents' problems and bring them effective solutions—fast. When the technophile traveler Scott Beale tried to pass through the security at the San Francisco International Airport on January 31, 2008, he was told to unload all of his electronic equipment for screening. He had to show his laptop, cameras, cords, and flash card readers individually to the security personnel as part of a newly instituted program.

Following his check-in ordeal, Beale wrote about his frustrating airport experience on his blog, Laughing Squid.[8] He noted that the new procedure could cause people to lose valuable equipment, not to mention extending lines and causing delays. The popular technology and lifestyle blog Boing Boing also picked on Beale's account and agreed that the ordeal could be too much for travelers.[9]

The Laughing Squid and Boing Boing posts coincided with the launch of the TSA blog Evolution of Security. TSA bloggers saw the amount of attention Beale's post was getting, looked into the situation, and shut down the program about a week after it started. As the TSA blogger Chris indicated in his February 6, 2008, post, the local TSA offices had set up the program on a trial basis to help identify electronic equipment that was not easily discernable through X-ray machines. The program was not put in place nationwide.[10] Following a brief investigation, the TSA stopped requiring passengers to take out all of their electronic equipment from their bags and responded to networking agents' complaints.

The Frozen Pea Fund

Besides bringing public affairs to the personal domain, networking agents can also carry personal stories into the public domain and instigate grassroots movements. When Susan Reynolds had a needle biopsy, she found the solution to easing her pain in pressing a bag of frozen peas on her breast. She took a photo of herself as such and shared it with her online friends through Twitter—a microblogging community connected through exchanges of 140-word messages.

Reynolds' sympathetic Twitter followers picked up on her example and started posting pictures of themselves alongside images of peas. One of Reynolds' Twitter friends, Cathleen Rittereiser, suggested donating the cost of two bags of frozen peas (about $5) to cancer research. This idea triggered another online friend, Connie Reece, to set up the Frozen Pea Fund. She rallied her network behind the cause to find a cure for breast cancer. All donations would go to the American Cancer Society's Making Strides Against Breast Cancer program, through the link on http://frozenpeafund.com.[11] Within five weeks of starting the fundraising efforts, Reece, Reynolds, and their friends had raised more than $8,000. Today, what started out as an idea posted on Twitter has become a nonprofit organization, with the mission of raising funds for breast cancer research, education, and programs around the world.[12]

Helping Earthquake Victims

Networking agents also rush to the help of those affected by wide-scale disasters. The needy may not even be able to get near their computers, but conscientious cybercitizens post items about the situation in affected areas and develop electronic badges and buttons that can be displayed in support of rescue efforts. They post these badges to their blogs and share the code for anyone who would like to copy and paste it to their social networking areas, joining their efforts. They help raise awareness and direct people toward Web sites that accept donations.

One example of such a benevolent act is what Ryan McLaughlin did following the tragic earthquake that struck Central China in May 2008. McLaughlin was a Canadian expatriate who lived in Suzhou, China. Through his blog, called The Humanaught, he reported on the state of affairs from the ground, inviting his readers to join him in the official three-day mourning period.[13] Using his creative Web design skills, he created an electronic badge that directed Internet users to charities assisting earthquake victims. Those who clicked through McLaughlin's "Help China's Quake Victims" sign found a page on Lost Laowai,[14] an online community of expatriates living in China, with specific instructions on numerous ways to help. The Web page included information on bank account numbers for charities and information on a text-to-donate campaign from China Mobile, and links to foundations that were rushing to help. The networking agent's electronic badge served as a reliable help line, bringing Internet users the most up-to-date information on ways they could contribute to relief efforts.

Tsunami Wikis

Networking agents' online posts and due diligence are not onetime shots in the dark. While opinions and conversations that are shared through face-to-face word of mouth rely on the memory of individuals involved in the events to stay on the public agenda before fizzling away, online word of mouth remains etched on Web pages. As search engines crawl over the Web and index online content, networking agents' opinions become easily accessible to Internet users who punch in key words associated with the post.

When online readers comment on a networking agent's post, link to it, or the agent updates the content, they bolster the entry. As a result, they push the post up in search engine rankings, making it easier to find. As the online buzz grows, long-tail discussions extend and networking agents' topics remain live.

The Tsunami Help Wiki,[15] a portal where multiple Internet users compile information regarding the 2004 Indian Ocean disaster relief efforts, and the Tsunami Help Blog[16] list continually updates information on resources to help the victims of earthquakes and tsunamis in the South East Asia region. The wiki includes a comprehensive list of articles, including those on aid agencies, help hotlines, news, and lists of people who are missing and/or have been found. The blog has been keeping tabs on every earthquake that occurred in the region since 2004. These Web sites, which are kept alive and enhanced by networking agents, exemplify how social media can long outlive events and remain relevant and accessible over the years while sustaining the momentum surrounding an issue.

Notes

1. "Global Internet Audience Tops 1 Billion; China Has Most Visitors,"*Marketing Charts*, January 23, 2009. The article refers to December 2008 World Metrix data released by comScore.
2. Dave Eberhart, "How the Blogs Torpedoed Dan Rather," Newsmax.com, January 31, 2005.
3. According to quantcast.com, as of January 2009, the Drudge Report received about seven million unique visitors per month.
4. Jeff Jarvis, Buzzmachine, www.buzzmachine.com/archives/cat_dell.html, June 21, 2005 (accessed January 19, 2009).
5. Vincent Ferrari, Insignificant Thoughts, www.insignificantthoughts.com/2006/06/13/ (accessed January 19, 2009).

6. Vincent Ferrari, Insignificant Thoughts, www.insignificantthoughts
   .com/2006/06/20/aol-apologizes-officially/; June 20, 2006 (accessed
   January 19, 2009).
7. Ferrari directs visitors to his blog entry about AOL customer service
   to a news clip on YouTube, called "Cancel AOL," www.youtube.com/
   watch?v=xmpDSBAh6RY (accessed February 8, 2009).
8. Scott Beale, Laughing Squid, http://laughingsquid.com/tsa-now
   -requiring-all-electronic-items-placed-in-bins-at-sfo/; January 31, 2008.
9. Mark Frauenfelder, Boing Boing, www.boingboing.net/2008/01/31/
   new-tsa-requirement.html; January 31, 2008.
10. The TSA Blog, "Evolution of Security," www.tsa.gov/blog/2008/02/
    hooray-bloggers.html; February 6, 2008.
11. Craig Colgan, "How Frozen Peas Started a Movement," Washingtonpost
    .com, January 10, 2008.
12. Connie Reece, "Frozen Pea Fund Kicks It Up a Notch,"*Media Bulls Eye*,
    April 2008.
13. Ryan McLaughlin, The Humanaught, www.thehumanaught.com, May
    19, 2008.
14. The Lost Laowai, China Expat Community Web site, www.lostlaowai
    .com/china-earthquake-how-you-can-help (accessed January 19, 2009).
15. "Indian Ocean Disaster Relief Portal," www.tsunamihelp.info/wiki/
    index.php/Main_Page.
16. The South-East Asia Earthquake and Tsunami Blog, http://tsunamihelp
    .blogspot.com (accessed January 19, 2009).

PART II

FINDING NETWORKING AGENTS

To find and befriend networking agents, read and listen to online consumer chatter in blogs, social networks, forums, and beyond. Sort through online conversation threads to see who is associated with whom. Understand who follows whom.

Connect with those networking agents who drive online conversations. One should fuel word of mouth by acting like these Web-savvy online opinion leaders. Create branded areas on Web sites where networking agents hibernate. Network to build an audience and establish your presence. Be authentic, transparent, and responsive to earn networking agents' trust.

3

How to Find Networking Agents

To draw attention to an issue, start a public debate, or make meaningful contributions to an ongoing online conversation, companies need to act like networking agents. They need to know and understand influential cybercitizens. They need to adapt to the networking agents' tools and tactics to create change.

Managing online word of mouth and its impact on a company's reputation begins with monitoring online conversations. Before taking a stand on an issue or deciding to join a conversation, companies should understand the online landscape in their industry area. They need to find out which topics online consumers discuss on a regular basis and the context in which Web-savvy folk mention their brands. To prepare for an effective dialogue with their online stakeholders, companies need to identify the networking agents who spearhead conversations related to their brand and the Web sites and areas where these conversations take place.

The following are essential questions to ask when monitoring online conversations:

- What are the topics of discussion in my industry area?
- What is the tone and context in which online consumers mention my brand?

- Who is fueling the discussions around my brand?
- Where are these online conversations taking place?

The first step for researchers who undertake online monitoring is to prepare a list of key words associated with the brand and the issue at hand. Key word lists can include product, company, and competitor brand names. The list can be supplemented with words consumers often use to describe the issues and events concerning the company and topics associated with the company's products. Adding common misspellings to the list casts a broader net for the research and helps retrieve additional consumer-generated media.

Tip

When making a list of key words for online monitoring, cast a wide net and include variations and misspellings.

The second step in the process is to determine how to quantify and evaluate online influence for the brand and company. Influence indicators can include volume of online posts and comments, the number of people an online source reaches, and networking agents' authority on a brand, product, or issue. Companies can expand this list with data on consumer traits and behaviors related to their products and services. For instance, a biotech firm may only be interested in cancer patients, while a food company may want to focus on moms. A movie distributor may want to speak with those who post film reviews and express their intention to watch films on a regular basis. Across any industry area, the basic premise of online influencer communications is to find those networking agents who regularly speak up, make recommendations, and change their peers' attitudes and behaviors.

Tip

Online influencers are more than Internet publishers. People seek and follow their advice.

The next step following online influencer identification is to start monitoring consumer-generated media about the product, brand, or issue. The easiest way to start the research process is to use free online tools, such as blog and message board search engines. While this approach allows researchers to merely scratch the surface in discovering the company's online standing, it helps assess the extent to which audiences discuss companies online and determine the need to conduct in-depth, custom analyses with the help of a professional research firm.

The following are three steps brands should follow to find networking agents' posts:

1. Prepare a list of key words.
2. Determine influence criteria specific to your brand, topic, and company.
3. Use blog and forum search engines to find relevant posts that fit criteria.

Blog search engines such as Technorati, BlogPulse, Google BlogSearch, and Icerocket and forum search engines such as BoardReader and Twing offer general information on the latest

Tip

Use social media search engines and read networking agents' posts to devise an online communication and reputation management strategy.

postings around a given topic area. Researchers can also delve into the ever-growing microblogging community Twitter by taking a shortcut with search engines, such as TwitterTroll[1] and Twitter Search, dedicated to this tool.[2]

Assessing Online Influence

Upon entering the key words into the consumer-generated media search engines, researchers can read through the results to trace conversation threads and spot the most prolific networking agents who are writing on topics concerning the company. Researchers can estimate the influence level of the networking agent by setting a mix of quantitative and qualitative criteria (as seen in Exhibit 3.1), including reach, relevance, authority, advocacy, and comments around the post.

Reach

A blog's reach refers to the number of unique visitors the Web site gets in a month. Some bloggers use counters to display the number of unique visitors coming to their site and the number of their subscribers. Many bloggers do not share their traffic information publicly or they do not track at all. If this information is not readily available, then researchers can use online

Exhibit 3.1 Assessing Online Influence at a Glance

Reach	How many unique visitors does the blog or forum area receive?
Relevance	Is the blog or forum dedicated to the topic of interest?
	Is the post about the topic of interest?
Authority	How many blogs and other types of Web sites are linking to the post?
	Do the networking agents have expertise in the area they are posting?
Advocacy	Does the networking agent make any clear recommendations to buy a product or act on an issue?
Comments	Does the post garner a significant number of comments?
	Do readers say they will follow the agent's recommendations?
Offline Roles	Does the networking agent have any offline roles or habits that would bolster their online influence and authority?

tools such as Alexa (www.alexa.com), Compete (www.compete .com), or Quantcast (www.quantcast.com) to retrieve visitor data about the blog site.

For instance, according to Quantcast, popular blogs such as the Huffington Post, Gizmodo, and Techcrunch attract millions of readers from around the world. Huffington Post reaches more than 11 million people with its professional-quality editorial, Gizmodo reaches more than 7 million, and Techcrunch has a global readership of about 3 million.[3] The majority of blogs and forums do not attract this much traffic. Neither their proprietors nor the online measurement systems capture smaller sites' activities. Yet these niche Web sites contribute to daily discussions in their communities and they speak to very targeted audiences. Therefore, companies need to pay attention to both quantitative and qualitative measures when determining the influence of a networking agent. Online influence is as much about relevance as it is about reach.

Tip

Niche blogs that appeal to enthusiasts may have a high concentration of networking agents among their readers.

Relevance

While it is imperative for a message to reach as many people as possible, it is also critical that it finds the right audience. The traditional media measurement methods are focused on reach. Ratings, impressions, and eyeballs are part of an approach to quantify the distance a message travels and the potential impact it has on audiences.

The new media order requires us to think of the quality of audience a message reaches as much as the quantity of people it touches. With the advent of social media tools, myriad cyber-citizens created their own Web pages to express their opinions and share their interests. The online medium's flexibility in creating and delivering content allowed for the proliferation of niche Web publications. Compared with general interest portals such as AOL, Yahoo, and MSN, social media outlets draw fewer but highly relevant audiences who gravitate to these outlets to meet others with similar interests and to find rare information that can help them find solutions and move ahead. Those networking agents, who claim expertise in a particular area and publish regularly online, speak to highly targeted audiences.

The relevance approach suggests that if, for example, a runner's story is featured in detail in a reputable running blog, it may be as noteworthy as if it were mentioned in one line on a general interest Web site. The running blog would relay the message to a core group of dedicated runners, while the general-interest Web site would disperse the message among a broad audience that may or may not care about running.

Messages that make the biggest impact through social media are at the intersection of reach and relevance, where they reach a high number of key audience members. A review of a new smartphone by a Gizmodo blogger, a corporate social responsibility story in the Huffington Post, or an article about a technology start-up on Techcrunch reach droves of audiences who seek such news and share the bloggers' interest areas.

Messages in relevant outlets that reach narrow population segments can catapult to mainstream news and reach the masses with the help of networking agents. These individuals search, create, and distribute their own news online. They talk, e-mail friends, and post their thoughts on the Web. They can dig up information from blogs and forums that speak to small interest groups and carry stories from these online nooks to wider circles. When leading social media outlets link to networking agents' stories and quote their insights, the agents' words can reach millions of online readers in a day. When traditional media take note of the buzz on the Internet, networking agents' narratives reach the larger population, transforming their personal stories and views from local to national news.

Authority

Networking agents' experience, education, and expertise contribute to their perceived authority. Similar to the academic system, where authors quote and cite previously published resources and add their comments, their peers in blogs, social networks, Twitter posts, and other online areas quote authoritative networking agents. Even traditional media outlets might refer to a networking agent's point of view as published in a blog. This is the process through which networking agents infuse information into word of mouth channels and ever-expanding social circles.

The Technorati search engine ranks blogs according to an authority score, which is based on the number of links pointing to a given blog. The higher the authority score is, the more that blog wields influence, or so we assume. The links pointing to the blog indicate that other bloggers consider the author an authority on the issue and find the topic worth referencing.

In addition to checking authority scores, researchers should pay attention to posts and blog sections where the networking agents reveal details about their background, experience, and areas of focus. The agents' attempts to compile independent, third-party resources to create a knowledge hub for others would also deem them credible and bolster their authority.

Tip

The following are some indicators of authority for networking agents:

- Personal experience
- Professional background
- Number of links pointing to their blog
- Research on a given topic (e.g., reference list of third-party sources)

A practical approach to create a list of networking agents is to decide which factors will play the most important role in determining authority. Researchers can place varying weights on the evaluation criteria, depending on the elements that are most relevant to their communication goals. For instance, some may choose to rank bloggers with Technorati authority scores of 100 and higher (i.e., bloggers who have at least 100 third-party links pointing to their posts). Others may decide that it makes most sense for their organization to speak with those networking agents who are not only cited often by other blogs, but also have a certain professional background and write on a given topic at least once a week. They may also want to add reach metrics to the mix and make sure the blog garners at least 5,000 readers per month. Using such a mix of quantitative and qualitative measures allows researchers to pinpoint which networking agents would be closest to their cause and most open to communicating with them.

Tip

Choose influence and authority criteria that match your campaign goals. Consider approaching those networking agents who are popular and knowledgeable about your topic.

Advocacy

The volume of conversation networking agents generate with posts, comments, and links is typically used as a proxy to determine online influence. Conversation leaders are those leading and sustaining much of the discussion on the subject by frequently posting their opinions, drawing in references, and responding to others' comments. Yet researchers need to differentiate between those conversations that are descriptive and those that contain recommendations or warnings. To identify those networking agents who are advocating for a brand, product, or a company, researchers need to look for those who are making solid recommendations, telling others what to do, and potentially influencing others' opinions and decisions.

MotiveQuest, a strategic consultancy that analyzes online consumer buzz, has coined the term "online promoter score,™" distinguishing between those mavens who are generating much of the volume on an issue and those advocates who make recommendations.[4] Similarly, when reviewing networking agents' posts, researchers need to look for calls to action as well as reader comments that indicate agreement or disagreement with the networking agents' points of view. This type of content analysis can provide researchers with richer context and information as they evaluate networking agents' influence. Studying online opinion leaders' recommendation patterns can also help in connecting online buzz with offline consumer behavior. Researchers can look for relationships between the volume of posts with positive recommendations on a product or calls to action on an issue and offline outcomes such as sales, signatures, and votes.

Tip

Note brand mentions in networking agents' conversations. Their recommendations are highly likely to turn into sales and drive action.

Comments

Among the criteria researchers can use to evaluate networking agents' influence, reader comments are the most difficult to capture. Many readers of consumer-generated media do not share their reactions to online posts. Some fear that their responses might be misconstrued, while others cannot think of anything to contribute to the discussion. Those who want to add their two cents to the discussion and do not mind speaking in a virtual forum may have to type in their user name and password and pass through the spam filter before being able to post their comments.

When a networking agent's posts garner a steady stream of comments, researchers can delve further into the conversations organically generated by these posts. They can then analyze the way networking agents' statements are received by their online audiences. Researchers can treat comments around a post as a proxy for engagement or impact on an audience. They can also observe if audiences agree with networking agents' suggestions and whether they indicate they will follow networking agents' advice.

Tip

Comments to online posts offer additional qualitative insights about audience behavior.

Offline Roles

Networking agents can be influential online and offline. Their Web posts are often linked to real-world connections, needs, and events. To build a comprehensive profile of their influencers and to have a clear map of the way their audiences consume, share, and disseminate information, organizations need to understand their networking agents' offline roles and activities as well. A networking agent's profile may vary depending on the issue or industry. Organizations looking to identify their own networking agents need to determine a set of criteria that encompass traits of activism relevant to their sectors. For instance, a local nonprofit may want to focus on the most dynamic and regular members of the Parent Teachers Association (PTA) or a church. A technology service provider may want to speak with professionals who make purchasing decisions for their companies. A clothing company might want to know about those who shop and recommend brands to their friends on a regular basis. While targeting intensive Internet users who delve into social media, organizations can expand their definition of influencers to include behaviors that show leadership, enthusiasm, and dedication.

Tip

Networking agents' offline roles and behaviors matter. Those who are connected in both virtual and real worlds can cascade messages across a number of circles.

In today's information landscape, listening to networking agents' buzz and including consumer-generated media in reputation management efforts is a business imperative. Reviewing online buzz using blog and message board search engines can give researchers a high-level idea of a brand's online standing. To conduct in-depth and scientific analyses of issues and topics networking agents and their peers discuss online, companies may need to partner with research firms that use proprietary software to drill down on consumer buzz, collect representative data, and conduct content analysis synthesizing mass amounts of online postings.

A networking agent's commentary can blossom into an online grassroots movement. New additions to online discussions sprout overnight. Links branch from small-scale blogs to larger forums, feeding online and offline word of mouth. As a survey by Brodeur and Marketwire shows, more than three-quarters of journalists use blogs to get ideas for stories. Almost 70 percent of journalists have favorite blogs they read on a regular basis.[5] Journalists scour through consumer-generated media for story ideas and check the facts. With enough momentum, networking agents can catch a reporter's attention, turn their online posts into mass-media stories, and reach even wider circles.

When marketers notice that online constituents are discussing their brands or issues relevant to their business, they should move fast to identify the influencers who are driving conversations. They need to find ways to appeal to those networking agents and speak with their online followers. Whether contributing to online conversations with facts or letting online consumers try products firsthand, marketers need a plan to earn networking agents' respect and thus harness their power.

Notes

1. www.twittertroll.com (accessed January 21, 2009).
2. http://search.twitter.com (accessed January 21, 2009).
3. www.quantcast.com (accessed January 21, 2009).
4. www.motivequest.com/main.taf?p=1,2,1,1 (accessed April 21, 2009).
5. Brodeur Blogging Survey, Brodeur and Marketwire, 2007.

CHAPTER

4

Tapping into the Power
of Networking Agents

Enlisting networking agents to support a cause or brand requires meeting them where they are in social media and maintaining an open, authentic, and ongoing dialogue with them. Drawing networking agents' attention and asking for their support in spreading news entail online customer relationship management strategies and tactics. Communicating with networking agents requires willingness to share, listen, and devote time—as in any other relationship.

Campaigns that involve networking agents cannot rely on one-way, one-shot messages. Organizations that want networking agents on their side need to find ways to introduce their brands and causes to these information brokers, solicit their feedback, provide them with the facts, answer their questions, and keep them abreast of their news. They need to keep their relationships with networking agents current to remain on the online influencers' agenda, to earn their endorsement, and to have their fingers on the public's pulse as they listen to conversations about their brands, products, and issues.

Planning to communicate directly with self-appointed newsmakers in a virtual environment that resembles shifting sand and changes overnight is a complicated business. Faced

Tip

Communicating with networking agents is a form of customer relationship management. It is a long-term investment to increase brand equity and customer equity.

with the challenges of reaching narrow interest groups using new online technologies, many organizations delve into social media and make their mark through trial and error. However, there are methodical approaches to identifying networking agents and establishing long-term relations with them. The following is a tactical plan to achieve these goals:

1. Screen and sample
   - Tap into consumer panels and customer databases
2. Build and invite
   - Launch a company blog, a branded social network, or microsite
   - Invite your audience to online contests, polls, discussions
3. Go where the networking agents are
   - Visit fan pages on social networks and tell them about your blog, social network, and microsite
   - Release a widget on Web sites your audiences frequent
   - Participate in blog and forum discussions

Screening for Networking Agents

After determining the criteria for Internet users who would qualify as their brands' networking agents, companies can screen members of a consumer panel to find individuals who fit the desired profile. The critical step in this process is to estimate the number of networking agents the company should tap and engage. As Exhibit 4.1 shows, a sample of 100 networking agents who are experts in a niche area is enough of a group to provide the company with meaningful insights. A sample of 300 networking agents or more would allow

Exhibit 4.1 Networking Agent Panels

Sample Size	Outcome
< 100 networking agents	Qualitative insights
100 to < 1,000 networking agents	Quantitative insights
1,000+ networking agents	Quantitative insights and market impact

researchers to conduct more in-depth, quantitative analyses based on networking agents' feedback. To create a larger impact in the marketplace and to distribute information to even broader populations, companies may need to contact and inform more than 1,000 networking agents.

Companies should also bear in mind that the main goal of communicating with networking agents is to make online influencers aware of brands, products, and causes and to let them carry the word to their circles through organic word of mouth. While mass marketing primarily focuses on reaching as many people as possible, online word of mouth marketing with networking agents aims to reach relevant populations that would find the concept at hand pertinent to their lifestyle.

Tip

Fire off online word of mouth campaigns by seeding select groups of networking agents with information and samples. Reach relevant audiences as your brand's networking agents spread news across their social circles.

Upon pooling a sufficient sample of networking agents, companies can invite them to try their products or review materials about an issue or a cause. In these panels, companies can encourage networking agents to share their opinions freely, conduct research to trace how word of mouth spreads from networking agents to wider circles, and understand the impact networking agents' words and actions had on other consumers' attitudes and behaviors.

The following is a systematic approach to engage networking agents:

- Determine criteria to identify networking agents who would be interested in your company, brand, product, or cause.
- Identify your own set of networking agents through a screening process.
- Invite your networking agents to review your brand, product, or your cause.
- Encourage networking agents to share the information with their peers.
- Circle back with networking agents to understand how they spread word of mouth and made an impact on others' opinions and behaviors—if at all.
- Respond to networking agents' questions and continue the conversation.

When Nokia launched its 6682 SmartPhone, rather than invest in a massive marketing program, it decided to interest influential bloggers in the product to create awareness and sales. Nokia enlisted Matchstick, a word of mouth marketing company based in Toronto, which screened and recruited influential bloggers and gave them the cell phone free of charge. The screening took into account bloggers' age, mobile service provider, popularity among readers, the frequency in which they updated their blogs, and the degree to which they were socially active and connected.[1]

Tracking the results, Matchstick found that each influencer spoke about the new phone to an average of 84 people, both online and offline. During a four-week period, at least 193,000 visitors to their blogs saw posts about the phone. In addition, 69 percent of the blogging influencers said they knew someone who purchased or was planning to purchase the Nokia products because of their influence on them.[2]

Tip

The power of networking agents is not restricted to the Web. They bring campaigns to life through online and offline communications.

Online word of mouth programs work across industries' product categories and audience groups, as long as they involve networking agents. The word of mouth marketing company BzzAgent invites online word of mouth volunteers from its network of more than 550,000 people to review new Web sites and post their opinions on a designated Web area call the Frogpond. To date, Frogpond members have posted one million comments and made nearly a half-million referrals about Web sites in areas as diverse as entertainment, car repair, charities, kids, and personal training.[3] In addition to their activity on the pond, the agents write about the sites they evaluate in their own social networking areas and mention them in face-to-face conversations, bringing the news about the Web site to ever-widening circles. BzzAgent marries the survey information it gathers from these networking agents with the comments they post on Frogpond and their Web site visit activities. As a result, the marketing company is able to tell the Web site owners how many agents visited their Web site, how many posts they wrote, what the networking agents' attitudes toward the Web site were, and how many referrals they made about the Web site.

When *TV Guide* wanted to reintroduce its brand to consumers and show them that they had far more to offer than channel listings, they turned to BzzAgents for a multipronged, offline, and online word of mouth campaign. As part of the campaign's digital component, *TV Guide* was featured on the Frogpond and members were encouraged to visit TV Guide's profile page, read a review about the Web site, and then click through a link to experience the Web site firsthand. The Frogpond Web site tools allowed these networking agents to share their opinions with each other, post the Web site link on their social networking areas, and provide direct feedback to *TV Guide*.[4] As a result of the campaign, more than 7,000 unique visitors from the Frogpond visited the TV Guide Web site and 60 percent of them clicked through to the Online Video Guide. The networking agents sent 1,300 e-mails referring their peers to the Web site.[5] Their conversations continued offline as well. The agents indicated that they were highly likely to recommend the Web site to others.[6] Eighty-five percent of the agents said they were highly likely to return to the Web site and almost all (95 percent) noted that they knew at least one other person who would like to visit the Web site.[7]

As seen in the Frogpond case, networking agents make recommendations in both online and offline conversations. They are savvy Internet users who can gather and share information using Web-based tools. Their stories and recommendations echo across their network of contacts through online posts, e-mails, and face-to-face and phone conversations. Their versatility in collecting and spreading information signifies that their words travel far and fast.

Tip

Follow up with your networking agents after a campaign to measure reach, word of mouth activity, and impact.

Recognizing networking agents' proficiency in using multiple communication channels, SheSpeaks—a word of mouth marketing company focused on women consumers—surveys its panel members about their online and offline conversations. First, the company asks women who want to join the panel a series of questions about their backgrounds, communication habits, and areas of interest. Using this information, it matches the panel members with products that might be of interest and use to them. Those members who receive an invitation to participate in a campaign and choose to join can contribute to open discussions on the SheSpeaks members' site. They post news about the products they are reviewing on their Facebook accounts and share coupons with their friends. Following the campaign, SheSpeaks surveys the participants about their online and offline word of mouth activity, tracing the trail of information from the panel to social media outlets and to peer-to-peer conversations.

The common elements in Matchstick, BzzAgent, and SheSpeaks's approaches are that they have a disciplined process for identifying and selecting the networking agents who will participate in the online word of mouth campaigns. They observe buzz activity as networking agents interact with a brand, use a product, and have conversations with their peers. Following suit, these companies measure the impact of word of mouth on the product's lifecycle and capture the nuances in the types of recommendations networking agents make.

Building Conversation Forums

Besides working with consumer panels to elicit and evaluate networking agents' opinions, companies can build their own online forums. They can provide networking agents and their peers with virtual meeting spots where these online audiences can congregate to gain new perspectives on a brand or issue and can discuss their thoughts and share personal reactions. These conversation forums, such as company blogs, discussion boards, and branded social networks illustrate companies' commitment to their online stakeholders. They underscore the organization's openness in receiving feedback, weaving consumer perspectives into new products and services, and guiding their customers through key decisions. The ongoing conversation between the company and its online audience takes their relationship much further and deeper than in a pure commercial transaction. It enhances brand equity. It helps the company earn its customers' loyalty.

Tip

Show your commitment to networking agents. Host the conversation by creating a discussion forum.

The San Francisco-based bank Wells Fargo reinforces its corporate identity with a blog, called Guided by History, which focuses on its history. The company speaks to students about financial responsibility through The Student LoanDown blog and discusses its new products and services on the Commercial Electronic Office (CEO) blog.[8] Wells Fargo teaches its customers about smart money management through its virtual world, Stagecoach Island, where it initiates virtual quests and holds bingo tournaments and sports-related social activities.[9] This section of the bank's Web site keeps visitors engaged with the brand for an extended period while highlighting financial topics in an entertaining way. The Stagecoach Island virtual world's fame has spread to Facebook as well. In keeping with its social media identity, Wells Fargo has released a Stagecoach Island application on the social networking site. Facebook users can download the application to launch the virtual world from their profile areas, create an avatar, and join the conversation. The company also keeps a branded video channel on YouTube, featuring an animation clip with Stagecoach Island virtual world characters. With its online and social media presence, the Wells Fargo brand spreads itself to areas where its audience lives, offers helpful advice, takes questions, and increases the number of touch points with its customers dramatically.

To facilitate conversation and to connect its vast group of employees in a virtual setting, the electronics retailer Best

Buy built a social network, called the Blue Shirt Nation.[10] The platform was instrumental in helping the company executives find clues on ways to improve customer service and marketing based on its employees' online chatter. From this, executives gained insights into which products customers liked or did not like. When deciding to remove some products from shelves, they referred to the buzz from Blue Shirt Nation.[11]

Within two years of its launch, the community gathered more than 20,000 members. Participating employees could see that their opinions mattered and their suggestions helped shape company policies. Besides giving employees a way to communicate with each other between shifts, the Web site significantly increased the number of employees who signed up for the company's 401(k) offering and helped Best Buy make constructive changes to its e-mail policy.[12]

Tip

Private online communities can serve as a sounding board. They can give marketers feedback about products and procedures. They can alert them to brewing issues.

Southwest Airlines created a dynamic blog, called Nuts about Southwest,[13] to serve as a hub for the company's social media activities and to connect its employees with its customers and fans (see Exhibit 4.2). As the blog's user guide indicates, the Web site's audience is half Southwest employees and half Southwest fans. Web site visitors are encouraged to participate in the community formed around the blog by registering on the Web site to rate comments and post photos and videos. The blog authors update it regularly. They share everyday occurrences at the airline with items focusing on holiday

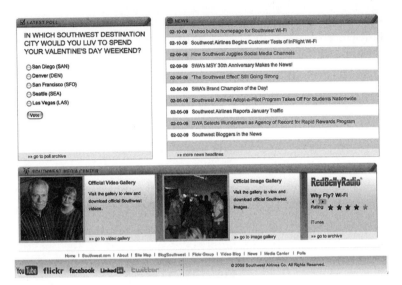

Exhibit 4.2   Nuts about Southwest

celebrations, how planes are de-iced, and how snacks are served in a whimsical tone, conveying the approachable, fun spirit of the Southwest Airlines brand. Nuts about Southwest also links to the company's pages on social networks, such as YouTube, Flickr, Facebook, LinkedIn, and Twitter. With its extensive presence in social media, Southwest Airlines communicates one-on-one with its networking agents and engages them beyond their typical points of service and gives them stories to tell.

Tip

Expand your digital footprint across multiple social media platforms and greet your audiences where they live online.

Tip

When authoring a company blog, match your brand's character with your writing voice.

PepsiCo's Mountain Dew brand has been cocreating and copromoting a drink line with its fans through its DEWmocracy[14] Web site. The soft drink brand first drew the fans to the Web site through a series of tasks and games to get the visitors to determine the basic elements for the next Mountain Dew line extension. Through the Web site activities, DEWmocracy participants decided on the flavor, color, name, logo, and label for the upcoming product. Mountain Dew Supernova, Mountain Dew Voltage, and Mountain Dew Revolution emerged from this experiment as the finalists. The products hit the shelves and the brand fans tasted and tried them firsthand. They returned to the Web site for a final vote-off, where they found tools such as badges, a video maker preloaded with images, and music segments and message boards to help them spread their enthusiasm about their favorite drink. Mountain Dew Voltage emerged as the winner. As Exhibit 4.3 shows, Mountain Dew keeps the DEWmocracy community engaged by encouraging members to promote Mountain Dew Voltage. While participants have fun, they also become brand ambassadors of the products they help create and of the company that listens to them.

Tip

Empower your networking agents by giving them the tools to construct their own messages and become storytellers.

Exhibit 4.3   DEWmocracy Voltage Web Site
© Mountain Dew.

While the creative ways in which companies employ social media platforms may vary, they share the same fundamental principle: These blogs, social networks, online video, and photo channels signify the commitment brands make to their internal and external audiences. The companies not only host Internet users in their branded Web areas, but they build and sustain mutually beneficial relationships with their stakeholders. They meet their networking agents, take their audiences' pulse and understand their needs, and evolve with the insights they gain from their conversations with networking agents.

Joining Conversation Forums

Companies can supplement their strategies to create momentum among a select group of influencers by joining networking agents' conversations in popular social media Web sites. For instance, the telecommunications giant AT&T uses the microblogging forum Twitter, the photo-exchange Web site Flickr, and the video network YouTube, besides spreading its news in areas where the networking agents hibernate. The company's online pressroom sends regular updates to ATTNews alias. Meanwhile, the company's ATTblueroom account on Twitter announces the latest music festivals and Webcasts that AT&T organizes, extending these marketing activities' reach. The company's small-business program also has a presence on the microblogging forum with the alias OnwardSmallbiz. Thanks to these targeted Twitter streams, the company can share its news with its followers and continuously communicate with hundreds of online stakeholders.

Fans of AT&T's commercials and those who cannot get the video clips of the songs from their sponsored events can obtain them on the ShareATT channel on YouTube. For more visual clues on the latest from AT&T, reporters, networking agents, and other consumers can visit the ShareATT photo stream on the photo-exchange site Flickr. AT&T's social media posts may not be reaching as many people as its TV commercials, but they are serving up-to-date news to audiences who like to receive their information online through forums where they can speak directly with peers and companies.

Tip

Brands that set up shop on popular social networking sites, such as Facebook and Twitter, need to differentiate their areas with compelling content and practical insights. They need to engage their audiences by participating in the conversation and leading discussions.

The social networking Web site Facebook, which catapulted from a college student network into a global Web site with more than 100 million members, also offers companies and nonprofit organizations ways to connect with their online audiences. Like any member of the Web site, organizations can create and manage branded fan pages on Facebook. They can invite their followers to virtual community discussions and share their news with them in written, audio, or video formats. Magazines such as *The Economist* and *Men's Vogue;* retailers such as Amazon.com and the GAP; technology companies such as Accenture, Intel, Apple, and Intuit; and nonprofits such as Teach for America, Greenpeace International, and UNICEF are among the many organizations that have set up shop on Facebook to meet their fans and recruit new ones through online word of mouth.

The Economist has decorated its Facebook page with news feeds, links to online debates, and a special comments area called the wall. It complements this content collection with online event updates and photo streams. Accenture's page serves as an internal discussion board, where employees from its offices all around the world post comments and questions. Apple Students' page delivers top listings from iTunes, the latest in entertainment news, and links to Apple's education site. In addition to facilitating conversation through message and discussion boards, the GAP uses its Facebook space to inform its fans about fun offline events it is organizing.

While Teach for America and UNICEF use their pages to introduce their causes to Facebook audiences with informational updates, photos, and videos, Greenpeace International takes a more vigorous approach in using the social media platform to reach new audiences. As Exhibit 4.4 shows, Greenpeace International streams directly from its YouTube channel to its Facebook page and links to other social networks and to its blogger news center. As a result, Greenpeace International's Facebook area carries a wealth of information blogging networking agents can read and publish.

Numerous companies, organizations, and nonprofits on Facebook find new fans through Facebook, as networking agents sign on and share their updates with friends, recommending that they also join their new group. For instance, the NBA's Facebook page has grown its population to almost 850,000 Facebook users who can receive news updates, compare favorite players of all times, and watch games live through

Exhibit 4.4   Greenpeace International Branches from Facebook
© Greenpeace International (www.greenpeace.org).

this area.[15] The Coca-Cola Facebook page, created by fans Dusty Sorg and Michael Jedrzejewski, connects nearly 3.5 million Coke fans on the social network. It is one of the most populated product pages on the site. The fan page's success has caught the attention of Coca-Cola executives in Atlanta. They embraced their fans' enthusiasm. "Mike from Coke" is listed as one of the page administrators, alongside Dusty and Michael J.[16]

With just one click, Facebook users can attach their name to a new cause, learn about events organized by a known brand, or find a convenient way to receive updates from a trusted news source. Facebook pages give networking agents the opportunity to broaden their networks by meeting others with similar interests. They raise their voices and find answers to their questions by participating in group discussions.

Tip

Widgets connect brands with their fans beyond Web sites and social networks. They can stream up-to-date information straight from brands to desktops and mobile phones.

Brands can also mount small-scale applications, called widgets, on popular Web sites to provide brief news updates and amusing distractions to Internet users. Widgets give networking agents something to talk about and share with friends, while turning their social networking profile areas and desktops into branded spaces. For instance, the self-publishing company Lulu.com's Storefront Facebook application allows users to display five Lulu books on their Facebook profile area. NBA's All-Star Ballot widget on Yahoo! gets users to place their bets choosing two guards, two forwards, and one center from each conference. The application loads up updates as players' scores increase. The Home Shopping Network's widget is a simple search engine that helps Mac users search for shopping items from their desktops. The widget takes online shoppers from their dashboard screens to the relevant area on the network's Web site, where they can find the kinds of items they have in mind. As networking agents download and place these types of widgets on their computers and social networking areas, they spend an extensive amount of time with brands and foment word of mouth.

Companies, brands, and nonprofits that build new online forums or join existing social networks start relationships with their networking agents. In doing so, they gain significant advantages in the marketplace. Whether launching a new product, advocating a cause, or dealing with an issue, organizations that foray into social media speak directly with their online supporters and reach wider circles of stakeholders through networking agents' posts, messages, and conversations.

Notes

1. Stephanie Rieger, "Word of Mouth Marketing with the Nokia 6682,"*Keitai: Mobility, Culture and User Experience,* July 7, 2006, http://stephanierieger.com/news-events/word-of-mouth-marketing-with-the-nokia-6682/. As Rieger indicates, Matchstick refers to the traits that suggest social activity and connectivity as key urban lifestyle characteristics.
2. "Getting Bloggers Onside," Interact with Bloggers, WOMMA Case Study Library (accessed September 1, 2008). www.womma.org/casestudy/examples/interact-with-bloggers/getting-bloggers-onside/.
3. Bzzagent, www.bzzagent.com/frog/FrogPond.do (accessed September 7, 2008).
4. "Re-introducing TV Guide through Online Word of Mouth," Create Pass along Tools or Objects, WOMMA Case Study Library (accessed September 1, 2008), www.womma.org/casestudy/examples/create-pass-along-tools-or-objects/reintroducing-tv-guide-through/.
5. BzzAgent shared this information through an e-mail interview.
6. The TV Guide Web site got a net promoter score of 51, which is considered above average for the category.
7. "Re-introducing TV Guide through Online Word of Mouth."
8. Wells Fargo, http://blog.wellsfargo.com/ (accessed May 30, 2009).
9. Wells Fargo Stagecoach Community, http://blog.wellsfargo.com/StagecoachIsland (accessed May 30, 2009).
10. Best Buy, www.blueshirtnation.com (accessed January 31, 2009).
11. Terra Hoskins, "Best Buy Employees Create Cheap Intranet," *The Ragan Report,* February 2009.
12. Adam Stewart, "The Success of Blue Shirt Nation," *discobeta,* March 4, 2008. http://discobeta.com/2008/03/04/the-success-of-blue-shirt-nation.
13. Nuts about Southwest, www.blogSouthwest.com (accessed September 1, 2008).
14. Mountain Dew, www.DEWmocracy.com (accessed September 1, 2008).
15. Facebook, www.facebook.com/nba (accessed May 24, 2009).
16. Facebook, www.facebook.com/coca-cola (accessed May 24, 2009).

CHAPTER 5

Earning Networking Agents' Trust

Upon identifying networking agents and finding ways to start conversations with them, companies need to earn these prized individuals' trust. As in any relationship, being reliable and candid are the prerequisites of a long-lasting connection between a company and its audience. Companies need to be responsive partners who add value to networking agents' lives. Those aiming to impress networking agents need to provide them with stellar service, quality products, and credible information.

When networking agents are satisfied with the products and services to the marketplace that deliver the utility and quality brands promised, they take it upon themselves to share their positive experiences with their friends and make recommendation with conviction. When they are dissatisfied, they issue warnings and send cautionary remarks through e-mails, blogs, and message board postings. They regard helping others as their mission and continue to talk about their negative experience in face-to-face conversations. Studies have shown that online influencers can share their experiences about companies and brands with 10 people or more.[1] The extent to which they can spread word of mouth depends on the size of their network, the communication tools they use, and the subject matter.

To maintain strong relations with their networking agents, companies need to keep their communication channels open, be responsive to incoming queries, and take their customers' pulse on an ongoing basis. They need to solicit and embrace feedback, stay in touch with their valued customers who want to hear from them, and bring fast and effective solutions to those who have less than ideal experiences with their products and services.

The following are three principles of earning networking agents' trust:

1. Keep the promise and deliver
2. Solicit feedback
3. Respond

There are various ways companies can show that they are genuinely interested in hearing from their customers. Some companies conduct surveys among customers on a regular basis to get candid feedback about their products and services. For instance, the fashion retailer Ann Taylor invites its interested customers to join its Ann Insights panel and surveys them about their shopping experience at Ann Taylor and other stores. The brand also seeks this select group of customers' opinions about upcoming product lines.

Tip

Brief surveys about customer experience can uncover new insights and draw networking agents into the research and development (R&D) process.

Accepting Reviews and Suggestions

Some companies give customers e-mail addresses, online forms, and hotline numbers, encouraging them to speak directly with company representatives. For instance, the consumer packaged goods company Colgate-Palmolive extends its Web site's "Contact Us" section into a customer relationship management area. The company directs online consumers who want to give feedback about its products to the Web site's consumer affairs section and asks whether they have a compliment, a complaint, a question, or a suggestion.[2] Depending on the type of product consumers wish to discuss, they are asked to fill out a brief questionnaire. They are encouraged to submit their comments to the company from the Web site.

Other companies allow their customers to share their opinions about their brands in public forums hosted on their Web sites. They give networking agents a public platform to post comments about their product- and service-related experiences and to let their customers evaluate different perspectives before committing to a purchase. The brick-and-mortar retail giant Wal-Mart and the online retailer Amazon.com present their inventory on the Web accompanied by authentic and real-time customer reviews. Following a similar approach, the jewelry company Zales, a $2.5 billion a year operation, has turned customer reviews and satisfaction scores into an asset. Partnering with the social commerce and technology company BazaarVoice, Zales added a Ratings and Reviews feature to its Web site. Using this Web tool, customers could rate each sales item and add comments and recommendations, informing others about their level of satisfaction. Following the implementation of this feature, Zales saw a 38.7 percent increase in online purchases of products with reviews. Products with more than five online reviews enjoyed a 101 percent increase in conversion from browsing to sales.[3]

Tip

Embrace the conversation. Exhibiting online word of mouth about products helps customers finalize purchasing decisions.

Exhibit 5.1   Tide's Virtual Meeting Area

The detergent brand Tide has also taken a network-based approach to engaging customers, seeking their opinions and stimulating conversations. Through its Web site, the brand delivers a combination of relevant product information, message boards, special offers, and fabric treatment information starting from its homepage. As Exhibit 5.1 shows, Tide's rich and engaging Web content, including articles about clothing care, fashion styles, and managing budgets, gives its online customers a reason to return and a place to state their opinion while learning from others' experiences. Video clips that

Tip

Be resourceful. Provide networking agents with useful information related to your products and transform your brand Web site into a destination for lifestyle news.

tout the brand's charitable initiatives, and that offer tips and downloadable discount coupons, turn the Web site into a virtual meeting spot. They encourage Tide's networking agents to start conversations and invite their peers to the site.[4]

Being Responsive

In earning and maintaining networking agents' trust, organizations must respond to their queries promptly. They must show empathy, expertise, and professionalism in handling their questions and in communicating that the company is working to bring solutions to their problems.

When networking agents run into difficulties with products and services, they often speak directly to companies through customer service channels or through online forums that are public. Companies can greatly reduce negative online chatter, increase customer satisfaction, and earn positive reviews by listening to their customers' voice and addressing their concerns as quickly as possible. When the online market CafePress.com receives a query from a Web site visitor through its "Contact Us" area, it automatically issues a ticket and promises that a company representative will reach out to the customer within 24 hours. The company representatives follow up with each customer by e-mail, phone, or an online community forum.

Tip

Addressing problems is winning half the reputation battle. Even if you cannot resolve product and service issues immediately, acknowledging networking agents' problems can reduce and neutralize negative chatter.

Brick-and-mortar companies and well-known brands also integrate smart listening tools in their Web sites to provide specific and in-depth responses to customer queries. Citibank supports its customers with service staff in its branches, as well as through phone and online feedback. Visitors to the company's "Contact Us" section on its Web site can send online messages to company representatives, access product and service information through pull-down menus directing them to appropriate Web site sections, and find phone numbers and mailing addresses. In August 2003, when Citibank customers were subject to a series of fraudulent e-mails about their accounts, the company took immediate action and alerted customers through direct e-mails and its Web site to warn customers about the possibility of identity theft. The "Contact Us" section continues to provide customers with tips on maintaining safe online transactions and how to report spoof e-mails to Citibank and the Federal Trade Commission.[5]

Providing Conversation Materials

In addition to menu options that organize information and direct customers toward solutions, companies can offer fact sheets, documents on frequently asked questions (FAQs), and online pressrooms to inform networking agents, improve their customer experience, and become part of their conversations. Ford Motor Company's social media–oriented pressroom[6] has more than links to relevant press releases. As Exhibit 5.2 shows, the Web site area displays photos, videos, and links to popular online automotive communities. The company encourages visitors to speak directly to Ford and connect with each other. It makes blogger networking agents' jobs easier by offering quotes, suggesting tags (i.e., online labels), and providing short copy that is easy to understand and relay.

General Motors Europe invites its visitors to join the online conversation through its social media pressroom[7] (see Exhibit 5.3). The company highlights the latest comments posted to its press releases, showing a word cloud of most frequently mentioned tags on the site.

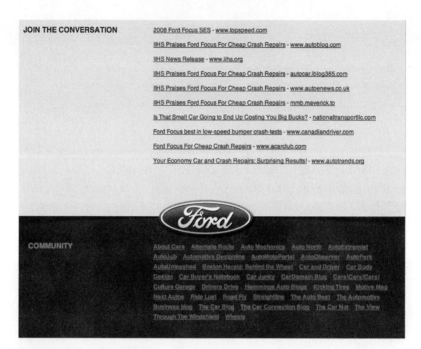

Exhibit 5.2   Ford Motor Company's Joins the Conversation

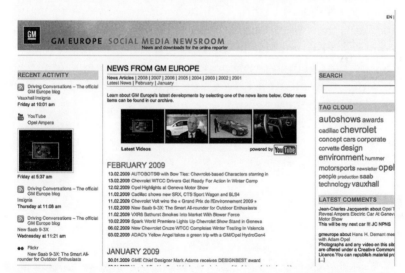

Exhibit 5.3   General Motors Europe's Social Media Newsroom

Tip

To be visible in social media, parse your information into pieces networking agents can grab. Offer videos and photos. Suggest tags. Provide content sharing tools.

Creating and hosting Web sites with conversational features is not an approach exclusive to corporations. Nonprofits and political organizations also delve into this space with similar tools and a strategic approach. One of the most engaging and action-oriented Web sites, which came alive thanks to the 2008 presidential elections, set the example for empowering networking agents and creating a grassroots movement online. Visitors to BarackObama.com got much more than news updates and could do more than watch compelling videos. On the Web site's activity center, visitors found ways to volunteer for the campaign and got tips on how to start conversations with anyone across America, including friends, family, and community members. They could customize their profile areas using a dashboard that helped them organize information and monitor their campaign-related activities. My.BarackObama. com was instrumental in coaching Web-savvy Democrats on how to start peer-to-peer conversations and to enlist others to join the movement. It served as a base for networking agents and helped them disseminate key messages.

By the end of the campaign, more than two million volunteers had created profile areas on My.BarackObama.com. They used the Web site to plan 200,000 real-world events,

Tip

To rally the troops offline, use social networking features that can help them find information, connect with like-minded people, and plan their activities.

form 35,000 volunteer groups, and publish 400,000 blog posts. Seventy thousand My.BarackObama.com users raised $30 million through their fund-raiser pages.[8]

Addressing Problems Head On

In addition to posting essential information in easy-to-access areas on their Web sites, organizations need to stay in touch with their networking agents and regularly update them about the latest developments concerning their business and social environments. These bits of information help networking agents share the latest brand-, product-, or issue-related news with their friends and family members while reinforcing their standing as public opinion leaders.

Apple maintains an ongoing dialogue with its customers and fans through its Web site, direct e-mails, and its wide web of customer services on the phone and in its retail stores. Apple computers come with their own e-mail program. On registering their computers, customers get their own Mac e-mail addresses. The company sends news about its product updates to its customers' Mac e-mail addresses and keeps broader audiences informed about its product line and company news through its Web site, Apple.com. When the company's coveted online storage system MobileMe had service glitches that interrupted the customer experience on July 16, 2008, the company decided to extend a month's free service to its customers affected by the problems. Apple customers learned about the company's offer first through e-mails sent to their accounts and through notices posted on the Apple.com Web site. The media picked up on the issue and networking agents buzzed about it on their blogs. While some were frustrated with the technical issues they were experiencing, they commended the company's efforts to do right by its customers. The Chicago free daily *Red Eye*'s Scott Kleinberg titled his post on iPhone, Therefore iBlog "Thank you, Apple: All MobileMe Applications Extended for 30 Days." Kleinberg noted that this was not the first time Apple was compensating customers for their service troubles and opened a dialogue with them.[9]

Apple continued to offer free services to make up for service glitches through September. MobileMe users were compensated for August and September 2008 service fees as well. To communicate directly with networking agents and other online stakeholders, Apple started a MobileMe status blog[10] with ongoing and timely updates about the service, related applications, and tips. Shortly after its launch, the blog changed its name to MobileMe News and started providing a steady stream of information to all networking agents at influential technology blogs like ArsTechnica, MacBlogz, and the iPhone Blog that covered Apple news. Today, Apple's handheld technologies are highly regarded for their design and functionality. Apple's direct, rapid, and transparent updates about the MobileMe service remain a successful example of how a company can manage relations with networking agents when facing issues and gain online leaders' trust by being forthcoming.

Tip

Timely apologies leave a long-lasting impression. They help mend tarnished reputations and garner networking agents' attention and support.

When speaking one-on-one with networking agents about product and service issues, companies need to speak with an authentic voice and first and foremost address their audience's needs. When companies notice questions and negative comments about their brands on blogs and message boards, the best approach they can take is to address the issue on the spot by providing clear information, offering a solution to the problem, and directing consumers to the appropriate online or offline helpline.

After dealing with significant cancellations and delays in a 2007 winter storm, JetBlue airline took bold steps to rectify its reputation in the public eye. David Neeleman, the company's CEO at the time, publicly apologized to customers.[11] The company issued a customer bill of rights, promising to notify customers about delays, cancellations, and diversions, as well as the reasons for the problems.[12] Today, in addition to keeping this document up to date and committing to the values it expresses, JetBlue uses dynamic communication tools, such as Twitter, to communicate with customers and fans regularly.[13] The company's representatives continuously send weather alerts, airport delay, and baggage policy notices on the micro-blogging forum to thousands of followers. They inform the communities about immediate business issues, explain how the company is attempting to solve problems, and, wherever possible, offer solutions to customers on the spot with useful links and news updates. While the company cannot solve all issues in virtual space, it earns customers' respect and gets a nod from networking agents for staying attuned to customer needs and being proactive.

In similar fashion, after being criticized widely for its poor customer service, the cable service provider Comcast has made real efforts to respond to dissatisfied customers by increasing customer service resources and taking grassroots action to speaking with its customers through these channels that facilitate rapid communication. Under the Twitter account Comcastcares, representative Frank Eliason, Director of Digital Care, has sent thousands of updates to anyone who mentions Comcast in their online postings. In addition, Frank trolls the blogosphere for any negative mentions regarding a Comcast customer experience and reaches out without missing a beat, encouraging outspoken customers to e-mail Comcast at We_Can_Help@cable.comcast. com or to bring the problem to the appropriate departments' attention at Comcast.[14]

Tip

Be available to speak one-on-one with your networking agents. Direct them toward company representatives on Twitter and live chat sessions, in addition to your phone lines and e-mail addresses.

Being Available

While it is imperative to be ready to respond when customers speak, it is also crucial to offer customers ways to get in touch with the company. As a company that prioritizes having a dialogue with customers, the home automation retailer Smarthome makes digital customer service part of the shopping experience. As Exhibit 5.4 shows, visitors to Smarthome's Web site can have a live chat with a customer service representative, in addition to sending an e-mail or calling the company. They can ask for help on lighting, security, and home entertainment products from the company's homepage.[15] The fact that Smarthome's customer contact channels are so readily available suggests that customer satisfaction is a top priority for the company.

Exhibit 5.4   Smarthome Chats Live with Customers

The fundamental principle in sustaining mutually trusting relationships with networking agents is to have honest and sincere conversations with them. Networking agents speak up to draw attention to issues and to protect others' interests. They do not shy away from expressing their satisfaction with products, loyalty to brands, and excitement about events that embody their values and passion. When a company hears networking agents indicate concerns, pose questions, or issue warnings, it needs to respond and make a meaningful contribution to the ongoing conversation. If networking agents are issuing recommendations, the company can direct these enthusiastic individuals to Web areas where the networking agents can receive ongoing news about their favorite brands and share them with their friends. Companies can engage these networking agents by recognizing their elite status among their audience and inviting them to vet and give feedback about new products and services. Companies that seek long-term relationships with networking agents, while being responsive communicators and reliable partners to networking agents, are bound to earn these public opinion leaders' trust—online and beyond.

Notes

1. *e*-fluntials® Studies; 2001, 2003, 2005, Burson-Marsteller.
2. Colgate,www.colgate.com/app/Colgate/US/corp/ContactUs/Consumer Affairs.cvsp (accessed June 17, 2009).
3. User-generated content increases all online product sales, plus 39 percent for those with reviews at Zales, Case Studies, Bazaarvoice, December 4, 2007, www.bazaarvoice.com/casestudy_pdfs/2008-02_rr_conversion_zales.pdf.
4. Tide, www.tide.com (accessed September 1, 2008 and February 2, 2009).
5. Citibank, "Learn about Spoofs," www.citibank.com/domain/spoof/learn.htm (accessed June 17, 2009).
6. Ford, http://ford.digitalsnippets.com/focus (accessed September 1, 2008 and February 5, 2009).
7. GM Europe, "Social Media Newsroom," www.gmeurope.info/social_media_newsroom/ (accessed September 1, 2008 and February 5, 2009).
8. Ellen McGirt, "Boy Wonder,"*Fast Company*, April 2009, pp. 62–63.

9. Scott Kleinberg "Thank You Apple," iPhone, Therefore iBlog, RedEyeChicago.com, 07/16/2008. http://weblogs.redeyechicago.com/iphoneblog/2008/07/thank-you-apple.html.
10. Apple, www.apple.com/mobileme/news (accessed February 4, 2009).
11. Jeanne Bliss, "Apology and Forgiveness," *Chief Executive*, October 29, 2007.
12. "Bill of Rights," Jet Blue, February 20, 2007 (retroactive to February 14, 2007), www.jetblue.com/p/about/ourcompany/promise/Bill_Of_Rights.pdf.
13. Dan Frommer, "Corporate Twitters You Should Follow—And Some You Should Avoid," *Silicon Alley Insider*, May 2008.
14. "Comcast's Big Push to Repair Its Image," *Philadelphia Inquirer*, April 19, 2008.
15. Smarthome, www.smarthome.com (accessed September 1, 2008 and February 5, 2009).

PART III

COMMUNICATING WITH NETWORKING AGENTS

Share useful information and newsworthy stories with networking agents to grab their attention. Consider their social environment and current events when constructing messages. Create memorable experiences to propel word of mouth.

Have an ongoing dialogue with your networking agents to establish mutually rewarding and long-term relationships. Listen to their concerns and ideas. Respond and deliver. Show them that you value their insights.

Follow up with your networking agents to tell them about the new products they helped create. Thank them for their charitable contributions. Give them credit for supporting your cause and serving as your ambassadors.

CHAPTER 6

Crafting Messages for Networking Agents

Faced with a plethora of information flowing from traditional and online channels, as well as conversations with friends and family, networking agents are as buried in marketing messages as the next person. Yet, as experts and interpreters often are, networking agents are adept at organizing information and noticing what is important. They look for substance. They want to uncover what has not yet been shared with a wide circle of people.

Those looking to become part of the networking agents' agenda and be quoted by them online need to deliver newsworthy stories. They need to offer an engaging process to share information and feedback and help networking agents boost their credibility by offering them valuable information to pass along to others. The following are the three fundamental elements of messages geared toward networking agents:

1. A newsworthy story hook
2. An engaging process
3. A value offer

Telling a Newsworthy Story

Networking agents are most likely to pass along messages that help tell an untold story and that offer counterintuitive facts. They confirm their newsmaker and influencer status by breaking news about new products and services that their friends must try, about places they must visit, and about activities they would profit from or enjoy. They need to tell a novel story to attract and hold their peers' attention. They need to know the details and see, test, and have the facts so that they are credible and convincing to their peers. The following examples show how a for-profit and a nonprofit organization successfully relayed their remarkable stories to networking agents.

We Can Blend Chuck Norris and Your Shoes

The marketing department at Blendtec (a maker of blenders, dispensers, and mixers for commercial and home use) posts videos online to demonstrate the power of its food processing products. The videos surprise and draw viewers as the company's founder and CEO, Tom Dickson, takes on a humorous persona and blends everyday objects using Blendtec products. Across numerous episodes, Dickson shows the power of his company's products by blending a rake, golf balls, glow sticks, a video camera, and an iPhone, among other objects.

The company started producing these videos and posting them on YouTube on a very modest marketing budget. While Dickson also blends common food products such as vegetables, chicken, and coffee, the appeal of his videos stems largely from the popular objects that consumers do not expect to see processed through a blender. The Blendtec video where Dickson blends an iPhone has been viewed more than 5.5 million times in one year on YouTube. Another video featuring a handful of plastic hero toys, including one of Chuck Norris, has been viewed more than 2.7 million times in one year. With more than three million channel views and 160,000 subscribers,[1] Blendtec's YouTube area ranks among the most popular channels across the vast video-exchange site.

Today, Blendtec complements its branded channel on YouTube with a microsite[2] called "Will It Blend?" Relying on the appeal of its online videos and dedicated fans, the company partners with other brands such as Nike to blend new, quirky items. With each demonstration showing a blender turning an everyday object into small particles, Blendtec representatives illustrate the strength of the product's technology. Viewers are left with no doubt about the product's power to process food items—whether in a house, store, or restaurant kitchen.

Tip

Stories worth listening and sharing are about the extraordinary. They combine elements of shock, surprise, and humor.

One in Six of Us Do Not Have Water

In 2005, New York–based fashion and entertainment promoter Scott Harrison spent a soul-searching year as a photojournalist aboard a Mercy Ship—a floating hospital offering free medical care—in Liberia, West Africa. On witnessing the extreme poverty and substandard living conditions of the thousands around him, he returned home with a mission. He would raise awareness about the water contamination issue in impoverished parts of the world and raise funds to bring clean drinking water to those in need. In 2006, he founded an organization called charity: water.[3]

The organization has striking photos and engrossing videos on its Web site. The staff explains the heart of the issue to potential contributors in one phrase:

> Right now, 1.1 billion people on the planet don't have access to safe, clean drinking water. That's one in six of us.[4]

People in the United States and other parts of the Western world may find it difficult to imagine what life is like in a developing nation they have not seen firsthand. The magnitude of the problem may be hard to grasp. Yet, the measure of "one in six" can be understood by anyone who knows how to count. Charity: water's message is simple and astonishing at the same time.

When Scott Harrison and his staff launched a new campaign in September 2008 to build 333 wells in Ethiopia, many contributors repeated this message as they announced their commitment and urged their friends and family to donate to the cause. Charity: water positioned the effort around the founder's thirty-third birthday and asked others born in September to ask their friends to donate to the cause rather than buying them less-than-useful birthday gifts. For their upcoming birthdays, September babies and their friends had the chance to make a difference in the world, instead of getting more stuff they may never use.

Visitors to charity: water's Web site found the tools they needed to make the call for help. Through the Web site's "Share the Story" section,[5] the organization gave donors the ability to send call-to-action e-mails to everyone in their address books. To help networking agents invite others with September birthdays, charity: water provided a downloadable "ask" kit. The electronic document illustrated the water deprivation issue with photos and numbers and showed that simple donations adding up to $4,000 could provide a village of 400 people with a well, giving these people a sustainable source of clean water for years.

The call for help made waves. Networking agents and their peers e-mailed, blogged, and sent Twitter messages. The charity staff promoted the cause. By mid-October 2008, more than 1,450 birthdays brought in about 6,000 water gifts. As a result, charity: water raised close to $1 million, which built 233 wells in Ethiopia, bringing clean water to more than 93,000 people.

The campaign's momentum continues as more socially conscientious networking agents and their peers invite other Internet users to donate. By the end of 2008, the organization had raised $8.5 million from donations and funded 1,247 water projects in 14 countries serving 640,000 people.[6] Charity: water continues to communicate about the campaign and fuel the conversation about the cause by sending donors electronic maps of the villages they have helped. The organization documents the creation of new wells with video clips and photos on its blog[7] illustrating how donors' simple actions produced grand results.

Tip

Numbers that deliver a poignant message and show a striking aspect of reality can help audiences visualize and empathize.

A startling statistic, a performance video, photographs from a personal journey, or insights on a social issue are among the types of intriguing messages networking agents would want to add to their knowledge bank. Regardless of type and format, the core of a message should be easy to understand and should allow networking agents and their peers to repeat and pass along. The message plays a critical role in conveying the value proposition. Paragraph-long corporate mission statements, data reams, or pages of explanations about the most frequently asked questions might help tell an organization's story and provide background information. However, it is best to give succinct explanations to networking agents about the differentiating and compelling aspects of a product, service, or cause.

Creating an Engaging Process

When informing networking agents about a story, communicators need to look for ways to create an engaging process where they help them to participate in a dialogue with the organization and have conversations with their friends and family.

If networking agents can take the story's basic elements and show how the concept applies to their lives, they can own the story and endorse it while passing it along. That is the approach Apple, New Balance, Veer, and CareerBuilder.com, among others, embrace.

Downloading and Touching Applications

In February 2006, Jeff Han, a research scientist for New York University's Courant Institute of Mathematical Sciences, presented an interface-free, touch-driven computer screen[8] at the Technology Entertainment Design (TED) Conference. With the news about touch-screen phones hitting markets, the esoteric technology started making waves in mainstream media.[9] In June 2007, *USA Today* published the Associated Press journalist May Wong's article "Touch-screen Phones Poised for Growth," indicating how the new technology was soon going to be a competitive feature on cell phones and would soon be in the hands of millions of people.

In July 2008, when Apple introduced its new iPhone 3G with touch-screen technology to the market, consumers rushed to stores. There was a key factor leading to iPhone's success, besides the strength of the company's marketing arm, its loyal fan base, and the buzz from early adopters who had bought the previous version of the phone in 2007. The Apple iPhone was not the first phone that enabled users to access the Web, share documents, send photos, and conduct online transactions on the go; there were other phones in the marketplace that carried similar functions at cheaper rates. Arguably, there were even those that were technologically superior to iPhone.

Yet the company turned the new product into a must-have for the masses by opening up its development process to the public and bringing networking agents into the adoption process. Independent developers who created iPhone applications offered consumers ways to mesh their Apple phones with their computers and everyday lives. Networking agents eagerly researched and talked about these applications. June 2008 data from the online measurement company HitWise showed that application-related searches were the most popular, following online searches about the new release and the brand name. The research firm Nielsen Online's buzz analysis for the iPhone showed that by the July 2008 launch, one in 100 new posts in the blogosphere was about the iPhone—more than for Presidential candidates John McCain and Barack Obama.[10]

Apple baked convenience, functionality, and consumer need into the product as the applications delivered entertaining and informational content to users. iPhone users could look up their location on maps, purchase tickets, bid on eBay auctions, read books, play games, and get the national news from the *New York Times* or the *Washington Post*. As a result, the phonelike minicomputer became a product defined by consumers. Users decided what their phone would do for them as they mixed myriad applications, songs, videos, and photos. Being an iPhone owner was highly engaging and rewarding.

The product's appeal showed in sales figures. Apple beat its projections for the fourth quarter in 2008, selling more than 10 million iPhones and surpassing industry analysts' expectations and projections in the midst of an economic slowdown.[11] While other brands followed suit shortly by introducing touch-screen phones to the market, Apple's iPhone labeled the category and commanded the lead with a remarkable product that connected Apple aficionados with their friends, families, computers, and the Web everywhere they went. Apple's success was in demonstrating its product's value to its networking agents and the masses, while creating an engaging process that drove

Tip

Customizable features enable shoppers to create their version of the product. They can then have unique stories to tell about their experiences.

customers to adopt the technology and to discover new ways to use their phones and create networks.

Running—For the Love of It

The Boston-based sports shoes brand New Balance's France division draws those customers who are serious about their love of running to its online running club.[12] The company, which had started at the turn of the twentieth century as a small arch-support maker, differentiates itself in the marketplace by offering men's and women's shoes that vary in width. Most shoes differ only in length. As a result, the brand became the preference of many who wanted to run or walk comfortably for extended periods.

New Balance's 2008 campaign, titled "LOVE/hate: This is the new balance," focused on joggers' irrepressible love of running, no matter how difficult it may feel to be dedicated to the sport. The French running club provides those with the passion for running with online schedules to track their progress, look for running mates, and attend nearby New Balance sports events. The Web site offers expert advice to runners to help them optimize their performance. There are three levels of membership: bronze, silver, and gold, with varying degrees of access to expert content. The levels offer VIP treatment at New Balance running events and other special offers. Web site participants are encouraged to recruit friends and earn points to proceed to higher levels of membership.

The points system encourages those networking agents who love to run to come forward and create their own running club with the help of the Web site. While New Balance facilitates communications between the networking agents and their peers, networking agents shape the recruitment process through one-on-one communications with their friends who might join them on the running trail. Because of the recruitment process and online and offline interactions with other runners and New Balance fans, the brand's networking agents are able to create a highly customized running club experience. While New Balance earns points for hosting the social network, the agents own their profile areas and create conversation on behalf of the brand.

Tip

Social networks focused on hobbies and professions enhance members' online and offline activities. These platforms bring like-minded people together, helping them set goals and track their achievements.

Creating an Image Online

Customizable Web sites give networking agents the power and ability to feature their brand on a virtual space and generate buzz among niche interest groups. Veer, a leading provider of images, fonts, and illustrations to creative professionals, created a truly interactive platform for networking agents to showcase their ideas and to connect with and learn from each other. To generate conversation among designers, filmmakers, and graphic artists, the company launched a social network called Veer Ideas.[13]

Besides setting up profiles and sharing portfolios with other visitors, Veer Ideas members can use the Web site's drawing tools and image bank to create their own digital environments on the spot (see Exhibit 6.1). They can share their aspirations on a communal blog and join contests where the Veer community decides on the best illustrations created on Veer Ideas with the Web site's tools. The Veer Ideas network takes Veer's commercial relationship with its fans to a higher level by engaging them with the brand while enabling them to do what they love the most—being creative and developing original content.

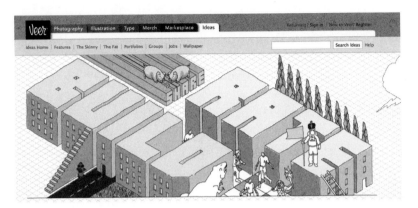

Exhibit 6.1   Veer Ideas

Tip

One of the biggest rewards for social network members is to have the space to publicize their creative work and get recognition.

Monkeying around at Work

Companies can also create engaging online experiences that extend beyond a particular Web destination and meet audiences where they are. For instance, an electronic message that travels from one e-mail inbox to another can reach a significant number of people if it tells a story that resonates with the public and if the recipients can customize it to reflect their personal style and preferences.

This is the creative approach the online job Web site CareerBuilder.com employed to generate buzz about the brand and to position itself as a category leader. The firm decided to harp on the common sentiments among dissatisfied and frustrated employees who spend much of their time complaining about their office environment. It created a message platform that played on the idea of a workplace with a bunch of monkeys.[14]

Visitors to the company's monk-e-mail page[15] could choose a monkey character, select its features and accessories, and upload their own voice to the newly created character using a microphone or phone. They could then send the message to as many friends as they wanted. The monk-e-mail page continues to entertain those who are bored with their jobs or simply have something to share with friends and are looking for a fun way to deliver their messages.

According to Oddcast, the makers of the technology behind monk-e-mail, millions of Internet users have visited and personalized CareerBuilder.com's message platform. Some 25 million unique visitors have sent monk-e-mail messages. More than 100 million monk-e-mails have been played. On average, users have spent 7.5 minutes customizing their monk-e-mails and interacting with the CareerBuilder brand. With monk-e-mail, CareerBuilder managed to brand the most commonly used online tool—e-mail—in an innovative fashion. The company drew networking agents' attention and enabled them to generate word of mouth on behalf of the brand.

Tip

Pick a theme to which many can relate and deliver your message with a creative twist. Say what everyone thinks about but hesitates to put into words.

Offering Value

Networking agents share stories to be useful to others, to make valuable contributions to public conversations, and, ultimately, to underscore their status as public opinion leaders. For networking agents, being in the know is akin to being rich in knowledge. If they can make a difference in the way others lead their lives, they can boost their credibility and reinstate their status as part of the knowledge elite. Those who have a newsworthy story to share with networking agents can galvanize word of mouth by highlighting the value proposition in their messages and calls to action.

Share Your Knowledge

Catherine Laine, director of communications at Appropriate Infrastructure Development Group (AIDG.org), a sustainability nonprofit that promotes environmental concerns, created a blog[16] to help promote her organization's initiatives in developing countries and raise funds online from microdonors. Laine and her staff update the blog with new research and case studies on a daily basis, keeping followers abreast of their fieldwork as well as developments in the broader sustainability community. They load photos from their fieldwork to Flickr and give frequent updates to their followers through Twitter. The AIDG blog monitors the green agenda and serves socially conscientious cybercitizens with an exhaustive list of links to key environmental sites and blogs. The blog also enables visitors to disseminate information from the Web site by adding their favorite AIDG postings to popular bookmarking Web sites such as del.icio.us, digg, Furl, and Stumble Upon (see Exhibit 6.2).

Erin Gifford is another blogger who shares hard-to-find information with her readers. She uncovers and distributes links to coupons and discounts from her Web site, CouponCravings. com. Almost everyday, she communicates with her audience about the latest deals on a broad range of products and services, including food, furniture, household goods, and cosmetics.

Gifford's blog commands a strong following that can be envied by established brands. Her practical advice and money-saving solutions reach about 14,500 subscribers. Close to 13,000 readers visit CouponCravings.com on a daily basis.[17]

Exhibit 6.2   Appropriate Infrastructure Development Group Blog

Tip

Do not just add to the conversation. Take it to the next level with new and rich information. Turn your followers into experts by sharing hard-to-find and unique facts with them.

Let Networking Agents Take the Stage

Spout.com, one of the largest movie communities online, serves its visitors with trailers, movie news, and reviews. The Web site has a vast inventory of films visitors can watch for free. The Spout team regularly publishes a podcast series called the

Film Couch, extending the film conversation far beyond their Web address with iTunes. In addition to encouraging its community members to rate movies, discuss viewings, and write reviews, Spout allows networking agents to create lists of films they have seen and films they would like to see or buy. These recommendations provide Web site visitors with a wealth of information on which movies to watch.

Spout.com fuels movie-related conversations with its group of movie mavens. These are movie aficionados who have at least five followers on Spout.com and who actively list, tag, and blog about movies on the Web site. Mavens recommend hundreds of movies in various genres and get tens of thousands of hits to their postings. With their profile areas where they display their contacts, reviews, blog entries, movie preferences, and their reader statistics, Spout.com becomes a dashboard for these networking agents who get to share their opinions with a sizable community of movie fans and lead conversations.

Tip

Encourage your community members to take the driver's seat. Give them the tools to promote their ideas and create groups.

Appeal with a Cause

Networking agents have the power to rally the troops and create their own communities around a cause in which they believe. During a trip to Argentina in 2006, Blake Mycoskie was struck by the fact that children in a rural village he visited did not have shoes to wear. These poor children had to stop frequently on the long walk to get clean water because their feet had blisters and infected cuts. On his return to the United States, Mycoskie started the TOMS shoes company, a moniker that stands for "Shoes for Tomorrow," making and selling the traditional Argentine *alpargata* slip-on shoes in the United States. The sales were tied to a worthy cause: For every pair of TOMS shoes a consumer purchased, TOMS would donate a pair to children in need.

TOMS is using the Web to show its ongoing efforts to bring its shoes to disadvantaged children around the world. The company's Web site catalogues the shoe drops in Argentina and in South Africa with videos. It solicits volunteer help to distribute the shoes and shows visitors the retail locations where they can purchase the TOMS *alpargatas*.[18]

The value in what Blake Mycoskie has achieved is indisputable. What is also noteworthy is how networking agents have taken the lead from him and continue to drum up interest around the company and its cause. In July 2007, David, a fan of the TOMS shoes, started a blog inspired by Mycoskie's initiative. On the blog, David repeated core messages from the TOMS Web site and showed how TOMS shoes gave 10,000 pairs of shoes to Argentine children and 50,000 pairs to South African children. The networking agent then asked other fans to send in photos and videos about their TOMS shoes. Today, the blog has turned into a vibrant community site called TOMS Shoe Fans.[19] It continues to highlight real-life instances of how TOMS shoes are worn around the world. As Exhibit 6.3 shows, the fan site turns the brand's aficionados into cause ambassadors by providing them with TOMS shoes widgets,[20] which they can use to post pictures of their favorite TOMS shoes models to their blogs and social networking profiles.

David informs the community Web site visitors of the latest shoe drop by linking to videos TOMS shoes crews film on-site and post on YouTube. Moved by TOMS's humanitarianism, David urges his audience to choose this particular brand. In his May 31, 2008, entry[21] he wrote,

I Love My TOMS Shoes Widget

Show your love for your TOMS Shoes with a "I Love My TOMS Shoes" widget for your MySpace or Blog. Choose your favorite pair of TOMS Shoes listed in the drop down and click "Generate Code". A preview of your TOMS Shoe widget will be displayed. CTRL+C will copy the necessary HTML code, so all you need to do is Paste the HTML code into your MySpace or Blog.

My favorite pair of TOMS are my [Red Wrap Boot ⬍] TOMS.

Generate Code

I Love My

TOMS Shoes.

Copy (CTRL+C) and Paste the following code into your page:

```
<div align="center"
style="width:135px;border:1px solid
#666666; padding:10px; font-
size:22px;">I Love My <br /> <a
href="http://www.tomsshoefans.com"
```

Exhibit 6.3 TOMS Fans Can Carry Their Widgets to Their Blogs and Social Network Profiles

Source: TOMSShoeFans.com.

After watching the four-minute video below, I honestly want to go out and buy about 100 pairs of TOMS Shoes. Nothing is more touching than a child's face, in my opinion. I think if you will watch this video with an open heart, you will likely be inclined to get yourself a pair of TOMS Shoes. How cool is it to know that just by buying yourself something, you are actually helping a child in need? I think that is VERY cool! Check the TOMS Shoes Story. TOMS Shoes are available at various places including Amazon.com, Shoes.com, and of course at TOMS Shoes.

David reiterates the brand's key messages, relays the story from his personal point of view, and links to retail locations for TOMS, making it easy for his visitors to purchase these shoes.

In 2008, TOMS Shoes pledged to give away 200,000 pairs of shoes. A search in Google's Blogsearch engine on TOMS Shoes returns hundreds of thousands of entries about the company's story. The posts include ideas from the company's founder, fans' accounts of how they love to wear their TOMS shoes, and praise from marketers' about the initiative. With the clear value proposition in TOMS's message, networking agents have embraced the company's message and are bound to help it reach its goals.

Tip

Be civic-minded and set social goals. Appeal to your audience with the opportunity to create noticeable change and make a real difference.

Whether making a concerted effort to earn networking agents' approval for creating remarkable products or hoping to get their support around a worthy cause, the first thing organizations need to do is to tell a compelling story. In today's cluttered information environment, the message needs to grab networking agents' attention, draw them into an experience, and give them benefits that go beyond the monetary value of a product. Networking agents need to become part of the story while sharing it with others. They need to join a movement and become leaders of their own right before urging others to follow. When writing messages directed toward networking agents, organizations need to share critical information, underscore the value they offer, and show how they can help networking agents make a difference in their communities.

Notes

1. YouTube, www.youtube.com/user/blendtec (accessed February 16, 2009).
2. Will It Blend, www.willitblend.com (accessed February, 19, 2009).
3. charity: water, www.charitywater.org (accessed February 19, 2009).

4. charity: water, www.charitywater.org/whywater (accessed February 19, 2009).
5. charity: water, www.charitywater.org/sharethestory.htm (accessed February 19, 2009).
6. Scott Harrison e-mailed this information to donors to charity: water.
7. charity: water http://charitywater.tumblr.com/ (accessed February 16, 2009).
8. Multi-touch Screen, http://multi-touchscreen.com (accessed February 19, 2009).
9. May Wong, "Touch-screen Phones Poised for Growth," USAToday.com, June 21, 2007.
10. "iPhone 3G Buzzing—Nielsen Online, Hitwise Issue Stats," MarketingVox.com, July 11, 2008.
11. Andy M. Zaky and Turley Muller, "iPhone Sales Surpass Q4 Consensus," Bullish Cross, http://bullcross.blogspot.com, October 6, 2008. This analysis is based on international mobile equipment identity numbers (IMEI).
12. Running Club, www.runningclub.fr (accessed February 18, 2009).
13. Veer, http://ideas.veer.com (accessed February 18, 2009).
14. Oddcast, www.oddcast.com/clients/monk-e-mail (accessed February 19, 2009).
15. Careerbuilder, www.careerbuilder.com/monk-e-mail (accessed February 19, 2009).
16. Appropriate Infrastructure Development Group, www.aidg.org/blog (accessed February 18, 2009).
17. Coupon Cravings, www.couponcravings.com (accessed May 29, 2009).
18. TOMS Shoes, www.tomsshoes.com/ourcause.aspx (accessed February 19, 2009).
19. TOMS Shoes, www.tomsshoefans.com/about (accessed February 19, 2009).
20. TOMS Shoes, www.tomsshoefans.com/i-love-my-toms-shoes-widget (accessed February 18, 2009).
21. TOMS Shoes, www.tomsshoefans.com/toms-shoes-argentina-shoe-drop -photos.html (accessed February 19, 2009).

CHAPTER 7

Reading the Message Environment

Creating a viral message does not have to be a shot in the dark. Motivating networking agents to embrace and circulate a message does not happen accidentally. Constructing a message that will resonate with audiences is part art, part behavioral science. Besides choosing the right angle and words, marketers also need to consider the environment in which audiences will receive their messages and take action. That means being aware of social norms and cultural codes, which shape people's attitudes and behaviors. Those who wish to push an issue or change public opinion also need to keep in mind the historical, political, and economic events that color and affect the messaging environment.

The following are the main questions storytellers need to think through and answer when developing messages audiences will listen to, discuss, and act upon:

- What are the attitudes of people in my target audience toward my industry, product category, and issue?
- Are there any political, social, or historical events that might influence these attitudes?
- Which elements in my story resonate with the target audience's culture?

- What would I like the audiences to do upon hearing my story?
- Does the message environment allow or enable them to take this action?

Audiences will embrace messages that speak to their needs and aspirations. If the message speaks to a current social, economic, or political problem and has utility and offers a solution, then audiences will be inclined to listen to and share it with others.

Messages that have successfully become viral phenomena online share some common traits. They consist of noteworthy, appealing content. They feed into public sentiment while challenging the status quo. To achieve this, they find out what is on people's minds. Meanwhile, they reveal new information. They tap into established networks and target sizable interest groups. Finally, these successful efforts involve messages that audiences can share easily, using do-it-yourself news distribution channels such as e-mail, blogs, and online forums. The following are the six steps marketers can implement to construct messages that resonate with audiences and spread far:

1. Tap into the public sentiment
2. Reveal the unknown
3. Challenge status quo
4. Infiltrate networks
5. Follow the audience
6. Make it easy to pass along and share

A review of some of the online stories that have become viral phenomena further illustrates what grabs audiences and urges them to pass along stories.

Tapping into the Public Sentiment

Political satire is a common theme that runs across popular Webisodes or online clips. Thousands embrace humorous content and share it with friends and family to liven up their conversation. This is especially true if the story ties into a social situation that affects them all. Humor, then, becomes a method for raising their voices and stating their opinions. The digital entertainment studio JibJab's animation video showing Al Gore and George W. Bush in a rap battle during the 2000 election campaign was one of the first broad-based hits on the Web. It was picked up by *Mad TV*, ABC News, and CNN among other media outlets. While working with corporate clients, the studio produced political parodies and released them online. Its 2003 Web hit featuring actor and governor Arnold Schwarzenegger, called "Ahnold for Governor," was showcased at the Sundance Film Festival. The studio's flash animation movie *This Land*, which mocked the 2004 presidential race, became so popular that it crashed the company's servers. When JibJab placed the short movie on the online movie site Atomfilms, the clip got more than one million hits within 24 hours.

The company's parodies are not limited to the political terrain. JibJab has released many short animation films poking harmless fun at well-known global companies and national news organizations. Their humor is based on extrapolating and exaggerating details many people see but do not voice or share unless with close friends. When it releases its animation clips, their points of view ring true with a considerable number of Internet users. Humor camouflages direct criticism of the established system. JibJab's clips give viewers the chance to implicitly communicate their own take on current affairs by sharing them with their peers.

Political humor can be instrumental in generating peer-to-peer conversations and pushing voters to take action. In the days approaching the heated 2008 presidential election, the civic action organization MoveOn.org released a fictitious news video from a supposed source called CNNBC, showing that Obama had lost the election because of one single vote. The story was structured so that video senders could insert their friend's name into the plot and customize the story. The story suggested that because their friend could not get up the day of the elections to vote, the election outcome was altered, affecting the whole country's fate. With this video, networking agents were able to give their friends two key messages: Everyone else is voting but you; and everyone will know if you don't vote.

The humorous take on the need to take civic action made waves. Online audiences used the video to send a message to friends and talk about an issue that was at the top of people's minds throughout the nation. Voting was critical during the tight political race that involved competing views on weighty issues such as the declining economy, national security, and overseas wars. Within this type of message environment, the video was sent to more than 11 million people in a matter of days. Moveon.org claimed it was going to 30 new people per second on October 31, 2008—four days before Election Day. The customizable video became a megaphone in peer-to-peer online conversations. With the push of the Send button, it turned many Web users into powerful networking agents.

Tip

To create a compelling message about a collective experience that has already been discussed in the news, focus on public sentiment. Understand people's reactions to current affairs. Become their spokesperson.

Revealing the Unknown

Not every online clip that has gone viral is as humorous as JibJab or CNNBC content. On September 12, 2004, an Internet user posted on a small message board called bikeforum.net a video showing how he could pick a U-shaped Kryptonite lock with a plastic BIC pen. Viewers flocked to the video. A couple days later, leading blogs, including Engadget, wrote about the issue. The story truly spun out of control when the *New York Times* and the Associated Press ran stories on the video on September 17, 2004, and fed the frenzy. A week after its first appearance, close to two million people had read the post. Kryptonite issued press releases, reached out to the media even more, and implemented a product exchange program that replaced 380,000 locks and cost the company millions.[1]

The Kryptonite is considered one of the strongest locks outdoors sports enthusiasts can use to safeguard their equipment. Many bicyclists in urban areas also rely on Kryptonite locks to prevent their bikes from being stolen. The online video showing how easily someone could open the lock challenged a well-established consumer belief that this brand of locks is durable and reliable. The *New York Times* article hit a nerve with many city dwellers who ride their bikes to commute to work, to exercise, and to travel across the city. If they could not rely on such hefty locks to secure their bikes, how would they be able to prevent theft? The news about the easy way to open sturdy bike locks without keys fed into one of bike riders' biggest fears. Without their bikes, they would be forced to find other ways of transportation to do basic daily chores and to get to work. While Kryptonite has recovered its reputation since the incident, the video clip remains an example of how information that has such a direct impact on people's lives can spread fast and far.

Tip

Traditional media channels can put the spotlight on facts known to a few online. They can draw people's attention to everyday matters, pointing out what has gone unnoticed.

Challenging Status Quo

Viral messages do not have to rely on isolated incidents or hinge on certain historical periods to spark interest and draw thousands of followers. A message can build momentum over time, as long as the cause remains relevant. Networking agents can challenge the status quo when they can find new information to benefit others and have the tools to fuel their advocacy efforts.

In 2002, when the animal rights organization PETA wanted to expand its supporter base with younger members, it launched a campaign supported by the Web site peta2.com. The organization started reaching out to younger Internet users with activities that resonated with this audience segment's online habits and social views. The campaign's slogan was "Question Authority." The Web site was equipped with smart tools that visitors could use to take immediate action—such as animal rights information, activism kits, and directions on how to join the peta2 street teams. Following these instructions, Web site visitors could join the forces of youth animal advocates.[2]

The organization started drawing traffic to the Web site by organizing online contests and giving away products that would appeal to its target audience while spotlighting its cause. Gift packages for online contestants included cosmetics verified to be free of animal products and signed memorabilia from music bands that support PETA. Offline, organization members attended youth-oriented concerts and events and recruited advocates by asking them to sign up for PETA e-newsletters. Because of these efforts, peta2.com grew by 900 new members per month and recruited 17,000 street team members onboard.[3]

To manage relations with its target audience on an ongoing basis, PETA expanded the campaign and established a presence for the organization on popular youth destinations online. In 2004, the organization created a MySpace page and followed this initiative in 2005 with a Facebook profile. These dedicated sections were far from static message boards. PETA staff members continuously updated the social networking areas with new and appealing content, such as links to interviews with musicians, celebrities, and athletes, as well as campaign updates and messages from PETA. The pages offered exclusive photos and videos to followers, informed them about upcoming PETA events, and gave them electronic badges they could post to their personal Web areas—carrying the word to their peer networks.[4]

The social network extension of peta2.com helped launch new campaigns targeting the youth audience and continuing to spark their interest in the cause. In 2006, peta2 announced the "Hug a Vegetarian Day" and created an online group to drum up conversation among supporters. Peta2.com members were asked to post pictures on the group's message board, showing them hugging vegetarian friends. These online efforts were supplemented by PETA's direct outreach to influential networking agents on MySpace and other organizations sympathetic to PETA's cause. PETA's live blogs on Xanga and LiveJournal communities, Flickr photos, and YouTube videos also directed attention to the well-orchestrated online campaign.[5]

By meeting its target audience where it lived online and delivering messages that resonate with young audiences, PETA significantly increased the number of its street team volunteers and peta2.com visitors. The organization's online efforts complemented its offline recruitment tactics. PETA used the MySpace profile area and its youth-oriented Web site as a launching pad for activism, bringing incidents of animal rights violations to their followers' attention on an ongoing basis. By the end of 2006, PETA was recruiting 5,000 street team members per month and the peta2.com e-newsletter was going out to 765,000 subscribers.[6] PETA's multipronged online campaign uncovered new audiences for the organization, while extending its message to a broader media base. The campaign, asking followers to question authority, appealed to idealistic youth who wanted to take action and make a difference in the world. PETA gave those who firmly believed that hurting animals was unacceptable the tools to construct their own messages, express their opinions, and spread the word on behalf of the organization. As the cause remained relevant over the years, peta2.com served as an online base camp where members contributed to a public debate, recruited peers, and picked up tips on taking action offline.

Tip

Understand the types of changes your audience wants. Use Web tools to alert them to ways they can improve their environment. Send them messages online, enabling them to take action offline.

Infiltrating Networks

Whether providing a two-minute entertainment break or making a claim about a powerful public figure, a message needs to resonate with the audience's attitudes, values, and aspirations to infiltrate through networks. The message needs to echo through the chamber of public sentiment and to touch a nerve and harp on existing sentiments.

In August 2007, Sporting Portugal—a leading Portuguese soccer team that needed to fill its stadium with fans during the new season—released a video[7] of the team's coach Paulo Bento making phone calls to the team fans. Visitors to the team's Web site were asked to submit their names and phone numbers before proceeding to the video. In the video, Bento was seen pacing up and down nervously, reviewing a list of players, and noticing someone was missing from the list. Next, he grabbed his phone to give a personalized call to the fan who had submitted his information. While watching the video, the fan's phone would ring and he would hear the message from the coach, saying the team needed him and he should come down to the stadium to show his support.[8]

Thousands of fans took the call to action seriously. Sporting.org, the Web site where the video was released, received 610,000 visits in two weeks. In the first couple of days of the campaign, 200,000 fans submitted their numbers to receive phone calls from Bento. The season ticket sales reached a record high in the first day of the season.[9] The audience's enthusiastic participation in the phone game worked, resulting in real support for the team. The message and the concept spoke to the fans who watched their team from the sidelines, discussed the games with their friends, and got emotionally involved with the wins and losses. The campaign tapped into their need to participate and drew them into the soccer experience.

Tip

Tap into preexisting groups whose members share an emotional connection. Give them the chance to participate in the game. Transform them from supporters into players.

Following the Audience

To accelerate word of mouth, communicators can direct their message to an existing community, which includes a high proportion of their target audience. This approach connects the idea and the organization behind the message with a group of people who have embraced a social identity and follow a pattern when consuming media, purchasing, or taking civic action. For instance, a company that delivers a message for mothers to an online women bloggers' network is more likely to find a relevant audience and reach more mothers than if it were to post the message on its Web site and hope people would find it through search engines or by remembering the Web site's address.

Balloon Time followed this approach to connect with female audiences online. The company produces helium balloon kits that can be used at birthdays, graduations, and baby showers, among other types of celebrations. To start a conversation with women who are likely to host such social events, the company reached out to members of the BlogHer community—a network of women bloggers featuring a publishing network of 2,700 bloggers that draws more than 10 million unique visitors per month.[10]

Balloon Time asked BlogHer women to post their party tips to a branded area it created in the special offers section of the network. The company also offered ways for these women to test and use the helium kits. Every day for two weeks, it offered a helium kit to a randomly selected BlogHer member who posted a party tip. The Balloon Time area on BlogHer gathered about 70 posts, as women kept coming back to the special offers section and posted new tips to be included in the brand's sweepstakes. The BlogHer women could follow a link from the special offers section to the Balloon Time Web site to print a $2 discount coupon for their next helium balloon kit purchase.[11] The brand also invited BlogHer members to follow Balloon Time's updates on Twitter, where it responded to its fans with personalized messages and offers.[12] These updates complemented online reviews from mommy bloggers who had tried the helium kits and had written long entries about their positive experiences, featuring Balloon Time photos.

The value of the initiative went beyond generating buzz among online women. Balloon Time's offer prompted many networking agents from the BlogHer community to come forward and talk about how much their friends and families enjoyed organizing parties and decorating with balloons. In addition to giving practical advice to its customers from its Web site, Balloon Time joined blogging women's conversations and helped to create a consumer-generated list of party planning tips. The extended BlogHer community read the authentic messages in the special offers section. In fostering such online conversations, Balloon Time positioned itself as a partner that helped women organize successful and fun social events.

Organizations that want to reach audiences online can fuse their messages into online applications commonly used by their target demographic segments and naturally tap into their peer networks. With its i'm Making a Difference initiative,

Microsoft connected a number of charitable organizations with its Windows Live Messenger and Windows Live Hotmail users. The participating organizations include Boys and Girls Club of America, The Humane Society of the United States, UNICEF, the Sierra Club, and the National AIDS Fund among others.[13] As part of this campaign, Microsoft's instant messenger and e-mail users could select the icon of the organization they would like to support and add it to their chat boxes and text areas. Microsoft tracked the advertising revenue generated by each user's conversations and matched a portion of it as a donation to the organization the user had chosen to support.[14] The users were encouraged to invite their friends to join the campaign, using the very tools that help them have daily conversations with their peers.

The initiative put the participating organizations in touch with people who may not have been able to donate before. The technological set up of the campaign made the act of giving as simple as chatting or sending a message. As a result, Microsoft users helped raise close to $2 million between March 2007 and November 2008.[15]

Tip

Do not wait for Internet users to discover the trail to your brand Web site. Launch your campaign at your audience's favorite online destination. Partner with other Web sites to extend your reach.

Making It Easy to Pass Along and Share

Many organizations turn to the Web to galvanize their programs. However, setting up shop online is not sufficient to draw the attention of the masses. In addition to preparing an online base where visitors can find information about a brand, product, or issue, it is also necessary to infuse established networks that share the values the brands and causes represent with the campaign's key messages. Once network agents review and approve the message, they can share the news with their network contacts and help generate widespread interest. To tap into the power of networks and help word of mouth agents share the message, it is necessary to adopt online vehicles that facilitate discussion.

Organizations can join ongoing consumer conversations and generate online buzz by using some smart services that help disseminate information in social media and bring their messages to networking agents' attention. For instance, understanding how bloggers like to consume information, the online news distribution service PRWeb takes a novel approach to issuing press releases. The company gives firms space online to post their press releases, testimonials, and photos and videos to tell their stories. Their editors review the written content to make sure that it includes key words that typical Internet users would plug into search engines when looking for information under that topic. The news area is also adorned with features that help spread word of mouth online. With one click, readers can forward the news to their friends, list it on a public bookmarking site such as Digg.com or Furl.com, and subscribe to receive e-mail updates from the company. PRWeb enables companies and organizations to deliver their news to networking agents and helps readers transmit the messages that resonate with them.

Following PRWeb's example, companies and organizations can set up an online newsroom with social media features that help disseminate information to multiple types of Web sites, including blogs, newsfeeds, social bookmarking Web sites, and social networks. If the organization doesn't have the means to build a comprehensive online newsroom with press release archives, photos, and videos, it can simply add either one of the AddThis[16] or ShareThis[17] widgets to their Web areas. These are free, small-scale but smart applications that allow

Tip

Let online followers add your news to social bookmarking Web sites. This tactic will help spread word of mouth about your brand, improve its search engine rankings, and introduce it to new audiences.

visitors to forward the Web site's address as an e-mail, post it as a link to their blogs and social networking areas, and add it to myriad social bookmarking Web sites with one right click.

Most online postings never make it to prime-time television, a news wire, or a national newspaper. Typically, they reach a handful of friends, family members, and accidental Web site visitors. Many branded Web sites, whether pushing a product or a cause, do not reach critical mass. Today, more than 133 million blogs[18] compete for the attention of Internet users. Online forums garner tens of thousands of postings. Thanks to affordable technologies and content management systems, companies and organizations can build cost-effective Web sites in a short period. These flexible and easy-to-use tools make the online space highly cluttered. Those aiming to break through the crowd and get their voices heard have to do more than rely on Web technology to disseminate their ideas.

A creative concept and a newsworthy hook are the fundamental elements of a word of mouth campaign. A story that is counterintuitive, entertaining, or shocking has the potential to become viral. The variable that makes the difference between stories that get lost and stories that catch on is a plan for distribution. To give news a long lifetime and to weave brands into daily conversations, marketers need to consider the way their audiences think, act, and receive information. They need to reach their audiences where they live online (or offline), motivate them to pass the story along by picking on the right cultural elements, and give them the tools to take action.

Notes

1. Nancy Flynn, *Blog Rules*, AMACOM Div American Management ASSN, 2006, pp. 153–154.
2. Michael Organ, "The Challenge," Chapter 11 Case Study, Issue Marketing, 2007, http://www.issuemarketing.com/case-study/peta2/challenge.html.
3. Ibid.
4. Ibid.
5. Ibid.
6. Ibid.
7. YouTube, www.youtube.com/watch?v=gQ42Kf_SFkE (accessed November 9, 2008).
8. Marketing Sherpa Viral Awards, 2008, www.marketingsherpa.com/viralawards2008/4.html (accessed November 9, 2008).
9. Ibid.
10. BlogHer Ads, www.BlogHerads.com (accessed February 22, 2009).
11. BlogHer Ads, www.BlogHer.com/special-offer-balloon-time (accessed May 25, 2009).
12. Twitter, http://twitter.com/BalloonTime (accessed May 25, 2009).
13. I'm Making a Difference, http://im.live.com/Messenger/IM/Causes/Default.aspx (accessed November 7, 2008).
14. I'm Making a Difference, http://im.live.com/Messenger/IM/Home/Default.aspx (accessed November 7, 2008).
15. Ibid.
16. AddThis, www.addthis.com (accessed November 8, 2008).
17. Share This, www.sharethis.com (accessed November 8, 2008).
18. "State of the Blogosphere," Technorati, 2008, http://technorati.com/blogging/state-of-the-blogosphere.

8

Keeping in Touch
with Networking Agents

Building and retaining an Internet presence requires time and commitment. When organizations launch online campaigns with the hope that their stories will spread like wildfire and become viral, they often limit the time period in which they will speak and be available to networking agents. This is largely a function of deadline-driven business processes where executives feel the need to show the beginning, growth, and final phases of a project. Yet generating positive word of mouth by tapping into the power of networking agents is an ongoing process that requires keeping in touch with these public opinion leaders and maintaining strong relations with them.

Marketers who build influencer programs often get the question "Why focus so much on a microsized group, when the goal is to create broad-scale change?" To justify the investment in maintaining ongoing relations with an elite group of stakeholders, consider networking agents' present and lifetime value. Networking agents adopt new products and spread news significantly faster than others. Companies that target their communications toward them can increase awareness and boost sales thanks to these opinion leaders who spread word of mouth, become advocates, and accelerate the adoption process.

A study by Libai, Muller, and Peres compares programs geared toward opinion leaders with those targeting average consumers. The researchers underscore the long-term value marketers can achieve by engaging the likes of networking agents. They show that engaging opinion leaders increases the long-term profitability of marketing initiatives by 6 to 14 percent, compared with programs targeting random customers.[1]

Tip

Campaigns fueled by networking agents reach further and yield more value than those initiatives that target audiences at large.

Need for Relationship Platforms

Networking agents knock on companies' doors and try to speak directly with them through their brand Web sites. They click through the "contact us" links and fill out forms, send e-mails, and make calls. While they may seem like hard-to-please or time-consuming customers who hog customer service channels, they present marketers with opportunities to listen to their constituents and enhance consumer relations.

Consumer feedback Web sites such as PlanetFeedback, Epinions, and ViewPoints flourish with networking agents' comments, who review and rate products. Smart companies look at these postings and respond—whether their audience is applauding or criticizing them. They create systems to maintain relations. They tap into these opinion leaders' knowledge and experience on an ongoing basis.

Keeping in touch with networking agents takes more than maintaining a list of a handful of outspoken online stakeholders. As in any relationship, it requires continuous, meaningful, and mutually beneficial communication. Organizations that want to maintain relations with their networking agents can follow traditional approaches, such as asking them to subscribe to e-newsletters and to participate in polls. Alternatively, they can orchestrate activities and manage communications with networking agents through online panels. Through these relationship platforms, networking agents can sample and provide feedback on new products or help support a cause. As brand and issue advocates, networking agents can turbo-charge campaigns by recruiting other buyers and prospects. Armed with novel information from organizers, panel member agents can reach out to their friends and families and ask them to join brand-supported activities.

Tip

Soliciting feedback from networking agents is only part of managing relations with them. For long-lasting connections, tell them how their ideas are shaping your business decisions. Make them partners in your cause.

The panels help companies and organizations stay on top of the mind. These online entities indicate to audiences that their opinions are valued. They help include networking agents in the product development and distribution phases. Through regular communications with panel members, brands maintain a connection with their networking agents and turn them into insiders. Meanwhile, the opinion leaders develop a deeper affinity for the brands, as they see their views make a difference in product development and service improvement. As the agents infuse their networks with the new knowledge they gain through panel activities, brands increase their share of conversations.

Sampling through Word of Mouth Panels

General Mills invites its passionate customers to join their word of mouth panel, coined as Pssst.[2] The online platform offers members the opportunity to receive online coupons and special offers. Members can also test new products and sign up to receive samples offline.[3] As General Mills indicates on the Pssst Web site, the company is interested in listening to its customers' feedback and opinions.[4] It hopes the conversation between General Mills and its customers, as well as conversations among customers, will promote the General Mills brands with customers' friends and family members.

Similarly, Kraft's online community, called First Taste,[5] draws customers to the company panel by telling them they can "try new products before anyone else." The site showcases blog entries from the Kraft team, highlights member profiles, and gives space to Kraft's networking agents to publish their product reviews and engage in conversations with their peers.[6] First Taste provides members with the tools to create customized pages where they can display their product preferences. With this online platform, Kraft learns about changing customer tastes and attracts valued customers who wish to be part of the product marketing cycle. Kraft earns networking agents' trust and support by providing them with premium product news.

Product Development through Online Communities

The software company Intuit, which makes the accounting and tax preparation tools Quicken, QuickBooks, and TurboTax, is another organization that is harnessing the power of online word of mouth with a community and maintaining relations online with its outspoken, proactive customers. With the TurboTax Inner Circle,[7] the company turns users into networking agents. First, it asks them to express their opinions about the product and share their experiences using it. Following suit, it pulls them into the product development process. The invitation on the community homepage reads:

> Tell us how we can improve our products and services. Contribute ideas for new features. Test-drive next generation software, and more.

The company transforms the feedback mechanism into a true dialogue. With an annual Webinar, it highlights how the ideas from the "Inner Circle" have contributed to product development and improvements.[8] In turn, the customer satisfaction and recommendations the online community generates help Intuit take the customers' pulse and remain attuned to their needs, while helping to grow business.

Fueling Word of Mouth on Popular Social Networks

Intuit does not wait for networking agents to find out about its products by visiting its Web site. It keeps engaging networking agents by reaching out beyond the physical parameters of its online community. In fact, the company has managed to turn a complex—and arguably dreaded—concept such as tax preparation into an approachable and fun topic by running a rap contest about taxes on YouTube. Intuit partnered with comedian Jay Mohr and enlisted aspiring and professional stand-up comedians to do routines about taxes, claiming "comedy is hard, TurboTax is easy."[9] The comedy contest was first run in 2006 and continued through 2008. The content is available on YouTube in a TurboTax-branded channel and attracts viewers daily. The video, where pro skateboarder Billy Marks plays Ping Pong games[10] and claims that preparing taxes with TurboTax is even easier, has received more than half a million views within eight months of its appearance on YouTube in March 2008.[11] Besides forwarding these funny videos to friends and spreading word of mouth about Intuit online, networking agents can also watch product demonstrations and listen to practical financial advice on QuickenOnline's Facebook page.

In 2009, Intuit launched a new campaign. It was led by an online video from singer Tay Zonday, called Freeloader Nation. From its campaign site, SuperStatus.com, Intuit regularly issued challenges to online taxpayers and asked them to respond by updating their status bars on MySpace, Facebook, and on Twitter.[12] The company entered contest participants into sweepstakes and gave prizes based on their responses and the number of followers who saw the updates. For example, to win a trip to New York and tickets to the *Saturday Night Live* TV show, fans were asked to write an opening for a *Saturday Night Live* skit about taxes, using the words TurboTax and SNL. They had to post their submission to their status boxes in 140 characters or less and draw their friends' attention to it. Intuit provided additional incentives to join the campaign and spread the word about it by distributing a free edition of TurboTax Federal through its Web site, SuperStatusContest.com, and its branded MySpace page, freeloadernation.com.[13]

With this campaign, Intuit highlighted its product's value and reminded taxpayers that TurboTax could get them refunds quickly if they file electronically. The contest was instrumental in transforming networking agents into brand ambassadors who spread word of mouth on behalf of Intuit by updating their status bars on popular social networking sites. Across multiple touch points, Intuit built brand equity. It maintained relations with its networking agents and stayed on its agenda.

Creating Multiple Touch Points

Traditional media companies can adopt blogging and networking platforms as well to find viewers online and start dialogues. Social media channels can help these organizations expand their reach and enhance their audiences' experience. In 2006, the public TV channel PBS launched a project called Remotely Connected.[14] The nonprofit organization invited a group of accomplished bloggers to review its programs and post their comments on the PBS Web site. The bloggers,[15] who are experts in a variety of topics, ranging from cartoons, literature, and technology to food, music, and politics, present viewers with alternative perspectives on programming, represent the voice of public opinion, and add to PBS content's richness.

The public broadcasting station's online community, Engage, is a true example of how an organization can generate discussion around its services and offer special content to those who want to have the scoop, while connecting one-on-one with its audience. In PBS's words, "The goal of Engage is to get the public more involved in public broadcasting."[16] The Web site, which claims to be an experiment in social media, features a series of blogs written by the PBS staff and those written by viewers who are commenting on PBS programming. Engage offers original online programming through live chats with experts, who discuss their subject matter and take online audiences' questions from the Web site. The gallery on Engage brings the nonprofit's various local broadcasting partners into the fold by highlighting the partners' presence on social media sites. This section contains a variety of social media content such as links to photos from the Nature program series on the photo exchange site Flickr, TV journalist Tavis Smiley's Twitter account, and highlights from Filmocracy, an independent film contest run online.[17] Thanks to the Engage Web site and Remotely Connected blogs, PBS partners create lively, rich, interactive experiences about the issues their programs tackle.

PBS's online initiatives are a far cry from static programming listings that only show titles and times. The Engage and Remotely Connected projects create an ongoing dialogue with viewers. They offer additional value to fans and allow them to share news about PBS content by forwarding e-mails and bookmarking their favorite pages. The top 10 searches section on Engage illustrates the audiences' taste and demand for PBS content by listing the most popular items that visitors search for on the Web site. With these dynamic features, PBS has removed the borders of the living room and managed to build a vibrant community of viewers that connect to PBS content and to each other.

Tip

After broadcasting and publishing your content, continue the conversation online. Invite your audience to share their views through blogs, chats, and comments.

Networking on the Go

Organizations can also reach beyond computer screens and use other Web-enabled devices to keep in touch with networking agents. Mobile communications offer ways to reach moving community members on the go, whether they are in their kitchens, at their desks, or on the road. In fact, President Obama's 2008 campaign relied on mobile technology to keep in touch with enthusiastic supporters and to assemble crowds at grassroots events. The campaign created an opt-in cell phone list and used it effectively to inform constituents with essential news and updates on locations of campaign events. At the Barack Obama Web site and at offline events, the campaign asked followers to send a text message to a dedicated short code to join their mobile communication list. They were thoughtful about not sending information to people's phones too often. They used this channel to deliver highly valuable information. The campaign disclosed the name of the much-awaited Vice Presidential candidate first to its mobile followers. Those who shared their phone numbers with the campaign got the information in their hands before the rest of the nation heard it through traditional media channels.

The campaign's accomplishment was more than delivering news fast. Adapting to mobile technologies, the Obama followers were able to connect with the campaign and with each other at local events. The campaign informed followers on its mobile list about the debate that would take place at the Howard University campus. Some Howard University students who came to the event told the campaign that they did not know about the debate until they received a text message.[18] The campaign's use of mobile technology maximized its reach and helped maintain and reinforce ties with followers who may have missed the news.

Tip

Mobile campaigns are truly permission based. They give networking agents the option to communicate with organizations. They help organizations speak directly with constituents through spam-free channels.

Guidelines for Long-Term Engagement

The tools an organization can use to keep in touch with and empower its networking agents can change depending on technological advances and social circumstances. Yet the need to foster a community after building an online presence remains essential. The following are basic guidelines for communicators who wish to stay in contact with their networking agents and reach broader audiences.

Ask for Permission and Create a Contact List

Whether inviting online customers to join a forum, to participate in a contest, or to send their feedback, communicate your motives clearly. Ask your audience for their permission before continuing to communicate with them. Once they opt in to be on your mailing list, then you can send them news, survey invitations, samples, and event information. Ask a few screening questions to identify those who might qualify as influential networking agents.

Communicate with Your Networking Agents on a Regular Basis

If you have invited consumers to an online forum and promised to bring them news and activities in exchange for their contact information, then they will expect you to follow up. The frequency in which you contact your list may vary by subject matter and your online audience's willingness to participate. While a good rule of thumb is to reach out at least twice a month, ask your community how often they would like to hear from you and stick to the schedule. With each communication, give them the option to change the schedule or opt out of receiving your messages.

Solicit Feedback

Make sure the communication is not a one-way stream. Whether through e-mail replies, online forms, or dedicated phone numbers, offer your audience ways to give feedback. When you hear from your networking agents, reply as soon as possible. If a speedy response or solution is not possible, acknowledge the query, start the communication, and report back frequently about your programs.

Encourage Peer-to-Peer Activity

Not all communication with your networking agents and their peers has to be handled by your company or organization. You may choose to host online activities that foster peer-to-peer conversations and that encourage exchanging ideas. Those networking agents with experience in using a product or service can help others seeking advice in the same domain. Those with strong opinions on an issue can step forward and take the lead in forum discussions. The group's collective intelligence can provide significant value and knowledge to members and moderators, including insights on audience attitudes and behaviors.

Celebrate Wins and Success Stories That Emerge from the Community

Create a structure where networking agents can share their stories and raise their hands to explain the secrets of their success. Honor those who win awards, share their stories, and participate in your community activities. Highlight their blog entries, introduce them to the community as experts, and reward them with points or branded thank-you gifts. These types of announcements will motivate the rest of the community to remain active, keep talking to you, and follow up with other members.

Bring Utility and Deliver Value

Companies need to offer more than branded virtual spaces to persuade networking agents to read their news, participate in online events, and visit the community areas on a regular basis. Networking agents have to see the value in joining these communities and receiving e-mail updates. Some companies offer prizes and chances to enter sweepstakes. Yet the most effective way to garner networking agents' attention, maintain relations, and be part of their conversations is to offer them premium information and firsthand experiences they cannot obtain elsewhere.

Networking agents seek knowledge. Make their time with you worthwhile. Be authentic and transparent in your approach. Offer them product samples and ask their opinions. Provide them with insider's information that they can take to their peers. Give them the opportunity to have a say in product development. Make it easy for them to connect with those who have similar interests. Help them learn from others' experiences. Networking agents will keep in touch, as they will find added value in following your news and joining the conversation.

Commit to a Long-Term Plan

Earning networking agents' trust and maintaining relations with them are long-term commitments. Most campaigns are geared toward creating a one-time spark to increase sales in a given period. To sustain excitement around a brand or interest around an issue, companies and organizations need to communicate with networking agents on an ongoing basis over an extended period. Keeping in touch with networking agents requires dedicated resources. Community managers, direct mail, and customer relationship experts need tools and time to construct messages, monitor activities, and offer insights and solutions to networking agents.

Marketers who want to reach the masses should first find those audience members who will be quick studies, volunteer to spread their enthusiasm and bring incremental revenue through referrals and recommendations. Networking agents adopt products, embrace causes, and propel messages to new heights. They lead large groups of people toward new ideas in the marketplace.

Networking agents who have developed relations with a brand would be ready to bring momentum to campaigns and fuel word of mouth when companies need to make announcements and want to draw audiences' attention. In times of crisis, these loyal aficionados would be hard-pressed to believe disparaging news. They would be willing to take the brand's version of the story to their networks. It would be in marketers' best interest to inform networking agents, invite them to share their opinions, and honor their relations for a long time to come.

Tip

Organizations that stay in touch with their networking agents build value. They protect and enhance their reputation and experience growth with online influencers' support.

Notes

1. Barak Libai, Etan Muller, and Renana Peres, "The Social Value of Opinion Leaders," Working Paper, Tel Aviv University, New York University, University of Pennsylvania, and Hebrew University of Jerusalem, October 2008.
2. General Mills, http://pssst.generalmills.com (accessed November 15, 2008).
3. Elaine Wong, "General Mills, Kraft Launch Word of Mouth Networks," *Brandweek*, October 5, 2008.
4. General Mills, http://pssst.generalmills.com/about.php (accessed November 15, 2008).
5. Kraft, www.kraftfirsttaste.com (accessed November 15, 2008).
6. Ibid.
7. TurboTax,http://intuitic.informative.com/intuitCTG/portal/home?source ID=101 (accessed November 15, 2008).
8. Creative Media,http://creativemedia.intuit.com/TY06/WEB/innercircle/ WebinarTY07.html (accessed November 15, 2008).
9. YouTube, www.youtube.com/user/TurboTax (accessed November 15, 2008).
10. YouTube, www.youtube.com/watch?v=2C-jDwHGsOI (accessed November 15, 2008).
11. YouTube, www.youtube.com/watch?v=2C-jDwHGsOI (accessed November 15, 2008 and February 24, 2009).
12. TurboTax, http://superstatuscontest.com/index.php (accessed March 1, 2009).
13. MySpace, www.myspace.com/turbotax (accessed March 1, 2009).
14. Public Broadcasting Service, www.pbs.org/remotelyconnected (accessed November 16, 2008).
15. Public Broadcasting Service, www.pbs.org/remotelyconnected/bios.html (accessed November 16, 2008).
16. Public Broadcasting Service www.pbs.org/engage/about (accessed November 16, 2008).
17. Public Broadcasting Service www.pbs.org/engage/picks (accessed November 16, 2008).
18. TechRepublican.com,http://techrepublican.com/blog/ipdi-top-ten-lessons -for-mobile-campaigning (accessed November 16, 2008).

CHAPTER 9

Delivering on Promises to Networking Agents

Responding to customer needs and demands is an integral part of a brand's reputation management and growth. There is a direct relationship between customer service, brand impressions, and business results. At minimum, brands need to deliver on their promises to customers with their products and services. To earn new business, they need to take their relationships with customers beyond transactions. Whether customers—especially the outspoken networking agents—are singing them praises or expressing their frustration and asking for help, brands have to respond and keep the communication channels open.

Networking agents are like consumer watchdogs. They make their demands known and they expect to hear back. Companies that deliver on their promises and fix problems receive high marks from these customer advocates. Networking agents make sure their recommendations reward the company and serve those who are looking to buy similar products and services. If the company leaves questions unanswered or fails to meet their needs, they let others hear their voices. They do so to warn and protect them from facing similar situations. In those cases, they cast their vote of disapproval, advising others not to buy the product. They cite the negative experiences they had when using the product or dealing with the company. Since they are highly regarded as knowledgeable people who are attuned to the latest trends, their peers pay attention. In these instances, dissatisfied networking agents turn off many potential customers and brand aficionados. Thus, to grow their business, organizations need to deliver on their promises and earn networking agents' approval.

Tip

Pay attention to dissatisfied networking agents. Their warnings can turn many customers away.

Turning Negative Buzz into Positive Buzz

When companies do not hear their customers' complaints, they put their reputation and stock at risk. Fearing negative comments, claiming that they are not representative of the overall customer sentiment, and turning a blind eye to them do not help. Companies need to hear what networking agents have to say. They need to seize the opportunity to improve customer service and salvage their brands' reputation.

Comcast Cares

It took a couple of networking agents to highlight the telecommunication company Comcast's customer service issues and spur a flurry of negative buzz both online and offline. When the cable company Comcast's technician was not only late to arrive at a networking agent's apartment but also fell asleep on the job, the whimsical customer captured the technician snoozing in his armchair with a video camera. Afterward, he posted it on YouTube for the video network's viewers to watch and comment. The video clip resonated with audiences and made millions of rounds on YouTube and personal e-mail accounts, making many laugh and some cringe at the thought of having their shortcomings displayed online.

Yet the true brand reputation crisis for Comcast erupted when *The Advertising Age* columnist Bob Garfield also became disenchanted with the telecom giant's service and launched his personal campaign against the company, reaching thousands of people. He wrote about his experiences extensively on a Web site he called ComcastMustDie.com.[1] Consumers who visited this Web site could entertain themselves watching a video of a prototypical customer going through five phases of depression while trying to deal with Comcast customer service. They could listen to podcasts where Garfield interviewed prominent guests about consumer rights. The Web site tied into a blog written by Garfield. Major media outlets such as the *New York Times*, the *Washington Post*, and *BusinessWeek* picked up Garfield's initiatives and covered the story and his perspective, citing his Web site. Garfield linked back to these stories, boosting his Web site's credibility and making his experience with Comcast reverberate across the Web.

Comcast managed to turn things around, transforming its image from a company that fails to deliver to one that listens and cares. Comcast tapped Frank Eliason to represent the company in social media as the Director of Digital Care. Using smart tracking tools, Twitter, and his blog, Eliason started addressing customer needs and issues, finding simmering issues, and responding to customers quickly. The speed in which Eliason addressed problems was the genius of Comcast's effort to rectify its reputation. Now there was an almost always available, sensible, approachable human face to the large company. Having been attacked for not delivering to its customers, Comcast started earning points by simply acknowledging issues, listening, and responding to customers and watchful networking agents.

Eliason was sincere and resourceful as he communicated one-on-one with disgruntled customers and networking agents.

When the former Comcast customer Michal Ciernak kept receiving Comcast bills for four months following the cancellation of his service, he took to the blogosphere. Michal started a blog called Consumer Complaint,[2] where he wrote about the ongoing correspondence between him and Comcast. When the blog Consumerist wrote about Michal's case and linked to his nascent blog, Eliason, a.k.a. comcastcares, posted a response to the Consumerist entry, apologizing to Michal and the broader online audience. Following suit, Michal received e-mail and phone responses from Comcast. Michal posted on his blog about Comcast's efforts to resolve the matter on his blog, acknowledging the digital care group's work.[3]

Tip

Approach dissatisfied networking agents with sincerity and address issues head on. Networking agents will acknowledge your efforts and help you turn negative buzz into positive.

Eliason speaks to business audiences as well. He presents the Comcast Cares case study at conferences and awes marketers who are looking to learn how to manage their brand's reputation online. During these presentations, the focus is not on the frequency and breadth of Eliason and his team's responses to customers. The number of cases he and his company have resolved is beside the point. Eliason is forthcoming about the fact that they may not be able to solve all problems online in an instant. Yet those who listen to his side of the Comcast story applaud the company for being open to communication and responsive to networking agents and other customers.

Today, Comcast has expanded its digital care suite to a team of digital care specialists. It has a number of customer feedback channels, including direct e-mail, customer forums, and communities. In addition to its corporate blog and Facebook page, the company's digital care team blogs and posts comments on highly reputable blogs such as Consumerist, reaching a critical number of networking agents. Meanwhile, knowing that Comcast has taken solid steps to address customer issues, Bob Garfield has announced on ComcastMustDie.com that he is moving his mission to another Web site, knowing that Comcast has taken solid steps to address customer issues. As a networking agent extraordinaire, Garfield continues his role as a consumer watchdog. He continues to follow companies and call attention to poor customer service cases on customercircus.net.

Norton Brand Advocates

Symantec Corporation, a global software company that offers security solutions, communicates with its customers through its Web site and other e-commerce Web sites that feature its products. The organization was challenged by negative reviews on e-commerce Web sites, which cited old product issues. Even after the problems were resolved, customers' criticisms did not subside. Symantec decided to find an effective way to speak and engage with customers who spoke about its products online.

The company deployed a survey and identified those loyal customers who might be interested in joining a campaign and representing the company to their peers. These extroverted networking agents were highly likely to recommend products. Symantec invited those who qualified to join the Norton

Tip

Look for your brand advocates among your loyal networking agents. They will trust you and share your story with their social circles.

Brand Advocates. By February 2009, the program included 7,000 customer advocates. The company hoped to increase the advocates group to 15,000 members by the end of first quarter 2009.

As Norton Advocates disseminated new information across their networks, Symantec reviews on e-commerce Web sites improved. For instance, within the first two months of the program's launch, the star ratings on Amazon improved by more than a star. Symantec also noted correlations between star ratings and sales volume.[4]

The cases of Comcast, Symantec, and other companies targeted by customers' negative remarks points to a single solution that can help companies manage their reputation online. Besides the obvious mission of delivering quality products and service, companies need to embrace all feedback—whether positive or negative. While common sense might suggest avoiding criticism, the age of social communications requires companies to keep up with negative comments and delve into social media to restore consumer confidence in their brands.

Companies that earn a certificate of excellence from networking agents thanks to dedicated customer service and high product quality can save dollars that would otherwise be spent on issue management. They can also boost sales. When organizations respond to networking agents' concerns and show their sincere interest in resolving problems, the agents deem their brands accessible, useful, and reliable. They talk and write about their experiences, drumming up positive word of mouth and influencing wider communities' attitudes and actions. Their recommendations turn into purchases.

Tip

Customer service is an integral part of online reputation management.

Online Reviews Propel Sales

Many companies are recognizing the value of authentic online customer reviews, as droves of Internet users are seeking and relying upon product and service information from other shoppers. An increasing number of online retailers are adding customer review sections to their Web sites. In November 2007, a study conducted by Vovici among 191 online retailers showed that, in preparation for the holiday shopping seasons, customer reviews ranked third in retailers' list of features added to their Web sites. Twenty-seven percent of retailers said they added faster checkout and order tracking functions, while a quarter (25 percent) of retailers reported that they added customer review features.[5] In the down economy of 2008, online reviews became all the more important for retailers to share with their customers. According to Vovici's 2008 survey on emerging technology priorities for U.S. online retailers, nearly 6 in 10 (58 percent) of the Internet retailers interviewed said customer reviews and ratings were a priority for them.[6]

The retailers' efforts to support their customers online are well worth the investment. A Rubicon Consulting survey conducted among more than 3,000 randomly selected Internet users found that word of mouth and online reviews were the most influential factors affecting consumers' purchasing decisions. Customers turned to the Web before and after making purchases. In fact, the Web was the second resource for customer support information after user manuals.[7]

Companies that embrace customer feedback have found that when they keep their customers satisfied and deliver on their sales promises, authentic testimonials drive business and fuel revenue. Small businesses featured on the popular review Web site Yelp.com enjoy the benefits of online customer testimonials. According to Yelp, Web site visitors who are passionate about a local business mostly post positive comments. For every negative comment on the Web site, there are six positive comments. Over the years, Web site visitors have written more than five million reviews. Eighty-five percent of these reviews give local businesses three or more stars.[8]

These genuine and candid posts help visitors who are looking for services in their areas find those businesses that deliver to customers' satisfaction. From car dealers and carpet cleaners to coffee shops, many small businesses featured on Yelp.com see an increase in the number of customers who find them through the Web site.[9]

Tip

Online reviews boost consumer confidence. They convert those shoppers who are on the fence into decisive buyers.

The pet product retailer PETCO is another company that saw a direct relationship between customer-generated comments on its Web site and its sales. Petco.com has offered a customer ratings and reviews feature since 2005. Seeing the online pet lovers' enthusiasm in sharing their experiences with Petco products on the e-commerce Web site, in May 2008, the online retailer added a question-and-answer feature to Petco.com, branded as the Answer Den. Using this feature, customers could ask questions to other Petco.com visitors. Those with experience and knowledge could post answers. These questions and answers are available for future shoppers to search through as they make their purchasing decisions. Web site traffic analyses showed that those customers who visited the Answer Den placed 100 percent more orders per session and had a 72 percent higher conversion rate from being visitors to buyers as compared with shoppers who did not engage with the Answer Den.[10] PETCO.com's community formed around the question-and-answer feature served as a testament to the company's commitment to its customers. The tool's flexibility enabled dialogue between customers and answered "why," "how," and "what if" types of questions that occurred to many shoppers before they made their final decisions to buy. The collective intelligence of the Answer Den was significantly more believable than blatant marketing messages pushing customers to buy. Networking agents among PETCO customers could browse through the answers to frequently asked questions and see how the PETCO products performed and delivered. The Answer Den encapsulated online word of mouth about PETCO products and turned buzz into a sales driver.

Tip

Include networking agents in your customer service team. Let them chat with other customers on your Web site. Help them share their experiences and make suggestions.

Authentic online reviews pay off in the offline world as well. According to a study conducted by the Internet audience measurement company comScore and the Kelsey Group,[11] online reviews affect consumers' willingness to pay for products and services, whether online or offline. Nearly one-quarter (24 percent) of Internet users said they referred to online reviews before making an offline purchase or reservation. The study focused on restaurant, hotel, travel, legal, medical, automotive, and home service industries. The results showed that online reviews led to high customer conversion rates for companies in these areas. Indeed, 41 percent of restaurant reviewers visited a restaurant and 40 percent of hotel reviewers stayed at a hotel after looking at online reviews. More than three-quarters of online reviewers across each of the industry areas said the online reviews had a major impact on their final purchasing decisions. Consumers looking for hotels (87 percent), travel (84 percent), and restaurants (79 percent) were most likely to cite the importance of online reviews on their offline purchases and experiences. They added that authentic customer reviews were more influential than professionally crafted ones. Almost all (97 percent) said they found the online reviews accurate, suggesting they had experiences similar to those reported online. Most notably, consumers indicated they would pay at least 20 percent more for those services that received top marks—excellent or five star—in the ratings systems.[12]

Tip

Many customers turn to the Internet before making a significant purchase offline. Online reviews can help seal the deal for an offline product or service.

Probe, Fix, and Communicate

Delivering on promises to networking agents is part customer service, part reputation management. Begin connecting with your networking agents and addressing customer satisfaction problems by reviewing comments posted online about your brand. If they are positive, user-generated comments can be business propellers, as seen in the Zales and PETCO examples.

Go through the messages addressed to your company on message boards and review e-mails that come into customer service and help addresses listed on your Web site. Solicit feedback by asking your customers their opinions on your products and services. Use open-ended questions, encouraging customers to elaborate on their perspectives. Answer questions as quickly as possible and address issues head on. Even if you cannot bring about immediate change, communicate how you are working to solve problems.

Tip

Satisfaction surveys and online buzz monitoring reveal customers' pain points. They also point to ways companies can fix and grow their business.

Apply what you have learned from your research to practice. To acknowledge customers' concerns and to demonstrate how their suggestions have been put to good use, show them your new and updated products and services. Specifically, reach out to outspoken networking agents who expect to be heard and who are ready to share your stories with their networks.

The following is a cohesive plan that companies can adopt to derive business value from customer reviews and other feedback:

- *Look in-house.* Review customer comments posted or sent to your Web site.
- *Cast a wide net.* Scan through customer reviews on third-party Web sites (e.g., retail sites, opinion sites, forums, etc.).
- *Be accessible.* Make it easy for customers to contact you through e-mail, online forms, phone, and mail.
- *Be proactive and ask for feedback* on how you are doing. Take the top complaints as direction for improvement.
- *Answer questions as quickly as possible.* Note that you heard the question and that you will reply.
- *Address issues head on.* Report on your progress as you work to resolve the problem.

123

- *Thank the networking agents* for their contributions to your business and show them how their opinions shaped your next generation of products and services.

Technical Assistance Research Programs (TARP),[13] a Virginia-based customer experience agency, has more than 35 years of experience in quantifying, optimizing, and managing customer experience for its clients. The firm's research confirms that those customers who complain but are satisfied with solutions the company provides end up being more loyal than those who do not raise their voices at all. The firm recommends soliciting complaints from customers and addressing those issues to improve the bottom line.[14] Likewise, direct dialogue with networking agents can turn them into loyal followers and active supporters. Their insights and direction can help companies take care of regular customers and appeal to new ones. When companies deliver on products and services they promise to customers, networking agents can drive sales with positive reviews and word of mouth.

Notes

1. ComcastMustDie.com, www.comcastmustdie.com (accessed November 21, 2008).
2. Why Simple Things Can Be Hard, http://consumer-complaint.blogspot. com (accessed November 23, 2008).
3. Why Simple Things Can Be Hard, http://consumer-complaint.blogspot. com/2008/09/comcasts-response-on-consumerist.html (accessedNovember 23, 2008).
4. Jeff Zabin, "The ROI on Social Media Marketing: Why It Pays to Drive Word of Mouth," Aberdeen Group, February 2009.
5. Ibid.
6. "Web Stores Score with Customer Ratings," eMarketer, September 12, 2008.
7. Jordan McCollum, "Word of Mouth, Online Reviews Most Influential in Purchase Decisions," Marketing Pilgrim, October 23, 2008. Rubicon Consulting's report, "Online Communities and Their Impact on Business," can be accessed at: http://rubiconconsulting.com/down loads/whitepapers/Rubicon-web-community.pdf.
8. Yelp.com, www.yelp.com/about (accessed May 25, 2009).

9. Geoff Donaker, Yelp.com, Word of Mouth Marketing University speech, Miami, Florida, May 13, 2009.
10. Sam Decker, "Customer-Generated Q&A Drives 72% Increase in Conversion for PETCO.com," Measuring Word of Mouth, Volume 4, WOMMA, 2008.
11. "Online Consumer Generated Reviews Have Big Impact on Offline Pur chases,"MarketingCharts.com, November 30, 2007. The comScore and Kelsey Group Study was conducted between October 12–28, 2007.
12. Ibid.
13. TARP Worldwide, www.tarp.com (accessed November 21, 2008).
14. TARP presentation at the Word of Mouth Marketing Association Conference, December 2006. For more details on the relationship between customer service and word of mouth, refer to *Strategic Customer Service* by TARP Worldwide's Vice Chairman John Goodman (AMACOM, American Management Association, 2009).

IV

CREATING ONLINE WORD OF MOUTH CAMPAIGNS

Create and join online communities to host conversations with networking agents. Talk about topics that matter to them. Trust your information with them. Give your networking agents the tools to share their honest opinions about your news.

Track networking agents' online conversations and activities. Make sure your messages reach as many people as possible among the relevant general public. Collaborate with networking agents to break stories, gather feedback, and build your reputation.

CHAPTER 10

Helping Networking Agents Spread Your Messages

W hether making simple everyday choices or deciding on lifetime events, consumers are increasingly relying on word of mouth, blending what they deduce from peer recommendations with what they learn from the media. Today, a comprehensive and effective communication plan needs to correspond with such consumer behavior and include methods to generate and measure word of mouth. Organizations need to feed their news to networking agents to be included in these volunteer spokespeople's recommendation sets. They need to facilitate word of mouth to be part of consumer conversations.

One way to draw networking agents' attention is to invite them to and host Web communities where they can mingle with like-minded people and speak directly with brands. Short-term goals and budget pressures force marketers to focus on single events and narrow periods when speaking with their audiences. Yet investing in online spaces where they can keep communicating with their constituents can yield multiple benefits and prove to be an ongoing source of growth.

Community areas where select groups of networking agents gather to communicate with a brand and talk to each other can help organizations gain customer insights, part critical information with these opinion leaders, and spread their messages through networking agents' online posts and conversations. Organizations may not have as much control over what networking agents write and talk about after reviewing their information, but they benefit from having third-party endorsements and feedback from these trusted word of mouth propellers.

Tip

Networking agents are the media. Online communities where these information seekers hibernate are instrumental in distilling news across numerous social networks.

To build a proprietary word of mouth channel where a brand and networking agents can have regular dialogue, marketers need to consider the Web community's features, methods to recruit networking agents, and the type and frequency of messages to send to their community. They also need to plan for the team they will need to put into place to moderate, join, and lead the community discussions.

The following is a list of basic questions to ask before launching a networking agent community:

- Where will we host the community and how will we build it?
- Who and how many will join the community? How will we recruit?
- What features will the online community area have?
- Who will develop and write the content to share with the community?
- What sorts of activities and incentives will stimulate the community and keep the members engaged?
- How frequently will we communicate with the community?
- How will we respond to the community's ad-hoc questions and comments?

Building Online Communities

Networking agent communities can live on the brand's Web site, in an area where visitors can sign up to become members and join the conversation with the company and their peers. Companies can also build dedicated Web sites where their online constituents can gather information, learn best practices from other visitors, and participate in live discussions.

IBM turns informational Web sites into dynamic virtual communities to foster communication and drive business. The technology company's developerWorks community Web site provides technical and hands-on information to developers looking to build applications using IBM and open-source tools. The Web site is frequented by more than two million developers a month who scan online libraries, watch Webcasts, and interact with other developers and IBM experts through the Web site's blogs, forums, and wikis. Whether looking to share code or test an emerging technology, developers benefit from the IBM community's collective intelligence.[1]

If companies do not want to dedicate internal resources to create and maintain such evolved communities, they can work with companies that build customized online communities and manage feedback panels on behalf of clients. For instance, Mercedes-Benz USA partnered with Passenger—a company that creates and maintains on-demand customer collaboration platforms—to launch an exclusive online community called Generation Benz, to target Generation Y customers.[2] The goal of the private online space was to allow the community members to interact and collaborate with the professional Mercedes-Benz teams. To join the forum, Mercedes-Benz fans had to be invited by current members. They signed up to share their opinions about the Mercedes-Benz brand and help shape the design and features of its future models.

Generation Benz allows the automotive giant to excite valuable customers about its products and enlist them before launching a product. The community puts the company in touch with its networking agents, signaling that the brand is eager to listen to them. The consumer feedback from the community Web site is sure to help Mercedes-Benz gain valuable insights about the attitudes and behaviors of its brand fans. Just as important, those Generation Y customers who are part of the co-creation process have much to share with their peers.

Tip

Online communities amass collective intelligence. Members' contributions can educate brands about customers' needs and spawn new product ideas.

Who to Recruit?

When inviting consumers to join communities, brands may want to focus on their networking agents. Creating a community of their most influential and outspoken online customers enables companies to take these opinion leaders' pulse and create waves with their news. In addition, recruiting community members who share interests such as owning a particular product (e.g., luxury cars, sneakers, or computers), a hobby (e.g., jewelry makers, running enthusiasts, or movie buffs), or a similar demographic background (e.g., moms, students, or boomers) can help foster a stronger sense of community and encourage invitees to recruit others like them. Brand communities do not need to include every type of customer, but they need to include those who are so passionate and interested that they will speak about the brand to the company and to their peers on a regular basis.

Tip

When inviting Internet users to join an online community, make sure to identify the networking agents among them. They will be your discussion leaders.

How Many Members to Recruit?

A fundamental question that comes up when developing such consumer platforms is how many people need to join the brand community. Brands need to speak with a large number of people over time to draw meaningful insights from consumer conversations and to be able to create noticeable change. They also need to be in touch with targeted groups of loyal, passionate customers who would be interested in passing along their messages.

Brand communities that can yield scientific, quantifiable insights have at least several hundred members participating in various Web site activities and answering polls. Those with fewer members can still give valuable qualitative direction to marketers. Their community discussions can serve as online focus groups.

In either case, brands need to be mindful of the demographic and attitudinal differences between their average customers and the types of people who would like to dedicate their time and energy to share their opinions, try products, and report on their brand experiences. Their community members will be more engaged with the brand than the typical consumer. They will also be more inclined to talk about the brand with their peers.

The power and scalability of word of mouth community engagements is evident in the case of H. J. Heinz's Ore-Ida. The frozen potato brand wanted to reach and appeal to those women who were looking for a practical way to prepare mashed potatoes. It needed to grab women's attention fast with its Steam N' Mash product. To achieve its marketing and sales goals, the brand partnered with the SheSpeaks word of mouth community, which boasts 100,000 women members.

SheSpeaks recruited 16,000 women from its community to participate in the Steam N' Mash program. Through SheSpeaks, Ore-Ida sent a free coupon to these networking agents to try the product and ten $1 coupons to share with their friends. As a result, the SheSpeaks community members generated one million conversations through face-to-face, phone, and online interactions. Forty-three percent posted about their experience on discussion boards, 39 percent e-mailed, and 27 percent mentioned it in social networks. More than one-fifth of the participants shared their stories about Steam N' Mash through their blogs. SheSpeaks and Ore-Ida tracked coupon redemptions: 82 percent of the women used the coupon for themselves and 89 percent gave the coupon to a friend. A survey of participating women showed that the brand's favorability and customers' intention to purchase increased significantly. Because of this community engagement, the brand sold more than 200,000 units.[3]

Tip

To gather meaningful insights from your online community, recruit at least several hundred members who fit your target audience profile.

How to Engage?

After determining the number and type of members to recruit for the online community, brands need to plan for the types of activities that will keep their online audiences engaged and compel them to come back to these designated areas. One of the main reasons why brands may defer the maintenance of their community to a professional service provider is the time and resources required to communicate with the networking agents who join their online community. After offering an online space to brand fans and public opinion leaders, the company has to work to keep the relationship alive and make its investment in developing Web properties count.

Affinitive, a word of mouth marketing company that builds custom social networks for brands, recommends engaging community members on a regular basis through e-newsletters, blog posts, and contests. The community moderators, who represent the brand, watch over the community's activities, answer networking agents' questions, create contests, and deliver news that is relevant to the community's purpose on an ongoing basis. They encourage participation by highlighting blog posts, forum comments, photo submissions, and contest wins from active members.

Similarly, experts at Communispace—a company that runs private online communities—recommend inviting community members to answer a few questions or participate in an online activity on a regular basis. Communispace recruits up to 400 consumers who are prescreened to meet their clients' criteria. Members of Communispace communities spend an average of 30 minutes per week sharing insights about their lifestyles, answering product-related questions, and exchanging ideas with each other, among other activities.[4] They appreciate the community's intimacy in voicing ideas, problems, and solutions. Most important, they know the brand is listening and valuing their opinions and taking their suggestions for product innovation and development. Thanks to their involvement in these branded private communities, the members become partners in companies' success. When they hear and see how their input has created an impact on business decisions and how they have helped a company they like find its course, the online consumers feel more affinity toward the brand, remain loyal, and continue to contribute to its growth.

Tip

Plan for weekly online activities to keep your community alive. Keep the dialogue going through polls, contests, and online events. Create a discussion calendar with evergreen topics, in case community discussions wane.

What Does Engagement Yield?

Conversations that spring from online communities have monetary value. These online hubs embrace loyal brand enthusiasts who bring new customers onboard. Companies get ideas for research and development from networking agents' comments and suggestions. Online communities help create new customer segments and business areas, as they facilitate dialogue between people with similar interests and backgrounds. The following are some examples of companies who are enjoying the benefits of engaging their networking agents through proprietary online communities.

Customer Loyalty and Incremental Revenue

The American Skiing Company wanted to enhance its relations with valuable customers and continue to connect with them online. It was looking for a solution to get its "All for One" season-pass holders to hear about each other's experiences and become aware of all the resorts they could visit in the Northeast. The company created an online community where members could get news about their home mountain as well as other resorts accessible with their pass.

When the American Skiing Company invited pass holders to the online community, the brands' online fans joined and contributed to the Web site content with their own ski-trip stories. They received information directly from company representatives and participated in online activities. As a result, approximately 3,900 pass holders posted more than 1,500 photos and videos, 3,600 comments, and 3,700 forum posts to the Web site. The "All for One" community helped cross-pollination among different resorts as the company's networking agents recruited other pass holders to the community Web site.[5]

The Intercontinental Hotels Group (IHG) also turned to an online community to generate word of mouth among current and potential customers. The company built an online community for its priority club rewards members and motivated these

136

individuals to spread news about travel deals. As part of the program, 150 IHG priority club rewards members received an invitation to earn triple points for every three-night stay between May 1, 2008, and June 15, 2008. They could have as many stays as they wanted within this time frame. The participants received a redemption code for themselves and three friends.

The effort resulted in 2,800 new registrations. Although the program originated in the United States, the loyalty program members' ties across networks brought customers from 30 countries to IHG. Participating customers amassed 7.2 million points. Meanwhile, IHG garnered $250,000 incremental revenue in six weeks.[6]

Tip

Loyal customers, who are invited to join special communities, help recruit new customers

New Products, Services, and Partnerships

Over the years, the greeting card maker Hallmark has forged strong relations with its networking agents thanks to conversations that brew in private online communities. For instance, members of the Hallmark Idea Exchange community gave the company numerous ideas for new products or making creative changes to existing products. They included bundling birthday cards, selling personalized cards, and creating journals that mark lifetime events, such as the birth of a baby, weddings, and graduations.[7] Hallmark has gone on to build communities for parents with young children, grandparents, and Latinas[8] to glean at these consumer segments' lives and to engage in conversations with them about how they celebrate special occasions and what their attitudes are toward giving gifts and cards.

Online communities can also be helpful to those faced with daunting challenges and are in need of counsel and support. The National Comprehensive Cancer Network's (NCCN) private online community connected first-time cancer patients and primary caregivers with the organization. The community, which complied with the Health Insurance Portability Accountability Act (HIPAA) regulations and strict confidentiality requirements, gave NCCN patient feedback and ideas to improve cancer patient support programs. Based on what NCCN learned from the community discussions, the organization developed new services, such as home treatment options, invitations to participate in clinical trials, and a custom partnership with the leading health Web site WebMD.[9]

Tip

Private online communities allow organizations to discuss sensitive issues with their audiences in a trusted, safe environment.

Conversation and Connectivity

Communities strengthen loosely formed social connections, introduce people who share similar characteristics, and bring them closer around shared interests. When Charles Schwab first launched a community for its traders, the discussion facilitators offered four conversation topics to members. Brainstorming around ideas and issues they cared about fueled a significant amount of conversation among the traders. The community spawned seven additional discussions and took on a life of its own.

The strength of bonds among community members was also evident in Charles Schwab's community for its affluent customers, with assets exceeding $100,000 invested through the financial services company. When the community for these high-value customers was disbanded, members tried to stay in touch with each other and continue their conversations by exchanging e-mails.[10]

Tip

Online community tools foster connections and help members make new friends. Carry your community's success to a new level by hosting offline events, meet-ups, and fireside chats.

How to Maintain Online Communities

Drawing networking agents to online communities and keeping them involved is as much a science as it is an art. While online communities help companies amplify word of mouth about their brands, many organizations find it difficult to maintain the communities. The Tribalization of Business study—conducted by the consulting firms Beeline Labs, Deloitte, and the think tank Society for New Communications Research—gathered responses from 140 organizations. They included business-to-business, business-to-consumer, and nonprofit organizations, which created and maintained online communities that ranged from 100 to more than 100,000 members. More than one-third (35 percent) of the respondents indicated that increasing word of mouth was the greatest value they derived from sustaining such communities. Respondents also cited building brand awareness (28 percent), bringing new ideas into the organization (24 percent), and increasing customer loyalty (24 percent) among the leading benefits of online communities.[11] The same study pinpointed the biggest threats to maintaining and growing communities: They were the difficulty in keeping members engaged (51 percent), finding enough resources to manage the community (45 percent), and recruiting new members (34 percent).[12]

Tip

Building an online community is not sufficient to create word of mouth. Companies that invest in such online areas need to appoint community moderators and brand representatives who have the time and skills to initiate activities and sustain conversations.

Companies investing in resources to design and build such online platforms need to think about training discussion facilitators and putting together activity calendars for their communities. They need to create a sense of involvement by keeping the community abreast of their news, giving them meaningful tasks, and showing them how their feedback has helped improve the types of products and services they bring to the market. The Web-based features in online communities help to keep the conversation flowing.

For instance, the Communispace community software gives companies the ability to set up brief surveys, have brainstorming sessions, post pictures and videos, and enable peer-to-peer contact through instant messages and e-mail.[13] Community managers play a pivotal role in the communications process by keeping an eye on members' activity levels. They recruit new members as some people stop participating. They take the lead in community discussions to draw in new members and encourage them to participate. Managing online communities and galvanizing word of mouth among its members are ongoing tasks that require brands to listen, share, and respond to their constituents.

Marketers need to have the following seven building blocks in place to create and sustain online communities:

1. When designing the community, determine focus and decide on Web site features.
2. Recruit members on an ongoing basis.

3. Dedicate time and resources to facilitating and moderating discussions.
4. Keep up the discussions with fresh news, polls, and activities.
5. Analyze content and activity to draw insights and set success benchmarks.
6. Respond to questions and comments from community members.
7. Provide incentives (e.g., premium information, branded goods, points, etc.)?

What Should the Incentive Be?

Branded communities house dedicated customers who are willing to give the company their time, thoughts, and efforts. The community managers may consider incentives to recruit members and to keep participation going. For instance, members can earn points based on their activity levels and redeem these points to get branded products from the company. Some panels offer their members the opportunity to donate to a charity of their choice, as a way to thank them for their participation.

For networking agents, the biggest draw in joining and remaining members of a community is not necessarily a monetary incentive. The communities offer them a chance to speak with like-minded people, expand their networks, and exchange ideas with their peers. They get the chance to be involved in developing and enhancing products and services for brands they use and love. As the brand communicates how the community members' opinions help shape the business, networking agents get the confirmation they need that their opinions matter. Their access to premium information from the brand helps them support their positions as opinion leaders in their networks. Their community membership becomes the biggest reward for their time and commitment.

Regardless of the amount and type of incentives companies may choose to give their community members for their time and participation, they should always instruct their members to disclose their relations with the brand when speaking with other consumers. The members should explain where and how they got their information. Whether they post positive or negative comments, their sayings must reflect their bona fide opinions. Such transparent and ethical communications instills trust in the brand, while spreading the word about its innovative ways to engage consumers.

One example of how a brand can empower networking agents and engage online audiences without monetary incentives came from the technology company Lenovo, a sponsor of the Beijing 2008 Olympic Games. Lenovo showed the world how its laptops could connect people through a blogger program. The company invited a group of athletes, who represented a variety of sports and countries, to blog during the Olympics and to be the "Voices of the Summer Games." Lenovo wanted the athletes to share personal, authentic stories with online audiences, while giving the fans an insider's view on how they prepare and compete. One hundred athletes from 25 countries agreed to participate in the program.

Lenovo provided the athletes with new Ideapad laptops and video cameras. The brand showed some of the athletes who had never blogged before how to communicate through this social media channel. The athletes were not paid in any way, other than receiving their machines. They were not asked or required to write about Lenovo. Their blogs were their own properties and responsibilities. While their entries pooled in a landing page supported by Lenovo, the brand did not edit their entries. The blogging athletes had to follow standard rules established by Google for its Blogger service users and they had to adhere to the IOC's (International Olympic Committee) content guidelines. Lenovo also made sure that the Voices program was communicated to audiences in a completely transparent fashion. The athletes sported electronic badges on their blogs, indicating to their readers that they were participating in Lenovo's Voices program.[14]

Because of the program, Lenovo was able to demonstrate its support for the athletes and show how its technology could help capture and share the Games' spirit. The blogging athletes generated more than 1,500 blog posts and received more than 8,000 comments from their fans. They created Flickr and YouTube accounts, sharing more than 840 photos and about 30 videos with the online Olympics audiences. Some of the athletes created Twitter accounts, sending 226 updates to their followers.

The athletes' stories echoed through social and traditional media. The Voices Web site was mentioned on more than 200 social media Web sites as well as the *Wall Street Journal, USA Today,* and *Times of India,* reaching a combined audience of more than 10 million readers. The Voices story spread further, as fans started clipping articles about the program online. Internet users reading about the Voices Web site listed 230 stories on the social bookmarking Web site Delicious.[15]

Tip

Networking agents do not need monetary incentives to spread word of mouth. Their currency is information. Always ask your networking agents to disclose their relationship with the brand when having product- or service-related conversations. When in doubt, refer to Word of Mouth Marketing Association's ethics code.[16]

How to Quantify Success

Conversations flow in and out of active communities. The buzz from these online hubs is not confined to networking agents' online meeting spots. Members, who seek information and take pride in being in the know, share the news with their friends and family and spread the brand's messages to their networks—online and offline. They make recommendations based on what they learn from the communities and what they experience thanks to their direct relationships with companies. Online communities that draw and inform networking agents create consumer promoters who can have authentic conversations about brands with their peers, face-to-face, on the phone, and online.

To obtain the full picture of their success, companies can track how their community members are actively participating in these branded Web areas and beyond. They can refer to their community Web sites' log files and use Web analytics tools to take the community's pulse and record the number of unique users who return regularly to the Web site to update their profiles, contribute to discussions, and cast votes on polls and contests.

In addition, companies can gauge their community members' word of mouth activities by surveying a representative cross-section of their online population. They can pose questions about these brand fans' likelihood to make positive recommendations and support their cause. They can ask about the number of people the members reach through their conversations when discussing the company's products and services. Brands can probe further about the quality and tone of those conversations, asking their members how those conversations propelled their peers to take an action, such as making a purchase, casting a vote, or relaying information.

Using the data they gather from the community Web site and surveys, companies can look for the connections and synchronicities between their online initiatives and their business growth cycles. The following is a list of measures brands can use to set benchmarks about their communities' activities and to determine their success.

- Number of active members
- Number of unique discussion topics and threads
- Volume of consumer-generated media (blog entries, videos)
- Participation in community activities (e.g., chats, polls, contests)

- Likelihood to recommend the brand, product, or service (Net Promoter Score)[17]
- Likelihood to support cause
- Number of people community members reach with their recommendations
- Actions community members' peers take following members' recommendations (e.g., sales, votes, signatures, donations, etc.)

As consumer trust in traditional media sources and overt marketing messages declines, companies and organizations will need to adapt to consumers' ways—listening to them and engaging them through non-mediated channels that enable authentic conversations. Online communities offer brands and consumers the space to have a real dialogue. They facilitate information and opinion exchange, giving networking agents access to insights unavailable elsewhere. Many communities sport a basic set of features that help users create, publish, and send content, such as polls, discussion boards, and photo and video display areas. While these Web-based tools enable networking agents to spread their messages, the quality of brands' relations with opinion leaders drive word of mouth.

Notes

1. IBM, "My developerWorks," www.ibm.com/developerworks/community (accessed March 15, 2009).
2. "Mercedes Benz USA and Passenger Launch Generation Benz Online Customer Community for Generation Y," Think Passenger Blog, November 17, 2008.
3. The details on this campaign were shared with the audience by SheSpeaks and Ore-Ida at the Word of Mouth Marketing University Conference in Miami, Florida, May 13, 2009.
4. Patricia Seybold, *Bathing Your Organization in Real-Time Customer Context, Outside Innovation: How Your Customers Will Co-Design Your Company's Future* (Collins Publishing, 2006). www.communispace.com/assets/pdf/C_Cli_Communispace_Case_Study_Outside_Innovation.pdf (accessed December 7, 2008).

5. "American Skiing Company—MyA41 Passholder Community," Affinitive, 2007. www.beaffinitive.com/clients/casestudy_american_skiing_company. html (accessed March 15, 2009).
6. "A Test with Infinite Possibilities," Communispace, Groundswell Awards, 2008, www.communispace.com/news/groundswell (accessed March 21, 2009).
7. Ibid. Seybold, p. 4.
8. Ibid.
9. "Walking in the Shoes of Cancer Patients to Improve Quality of Life," Client Story, National Comprehensive Cancer Network®, Communispace, www.communispace.com/assets/pdf/C_Cli_casestudy_nccn_final.pdf (accessed 03/21/09).
10. Ibid. Seybold, p. 12.
11. Tribalization of Business Survey, Beeline, Deloitte, and the Society of New Communications Research, 2008.
12. Ibid.
13. "Listening to the Heart: How Hallmark Is Creating Customer Communities with Communispace," The Abardeen Group, p. 2, 2003. www.communispace.com/assets/pdf/C_Cli_Aberdeen_Marketing_BP_ Report_-_Hallmark_Case_Study.pdf (accessed December 7, 2008).
14. Lenovo, "Voices of the Summer Games," http://summergames.lenovo .com.
15. These results were presented at the Word of Mouth Marketing university conference in Miami, Florida, May 13, 2009.
16. Word of Mouth Marketing Association, "Ethics Code,"http://womma. org/ethicscode (accessed May 3, 2009).
17. Net Promotoer Score®—a metric developed by Satmetrix Bain & Company's Fred Reicheld—shows the positive relationship between consumers' likelihood to recommend a product or service and the company's growth. In other words, the more the company's customers are likely to recommend its products and services, the more likely the company is to attain sustainable growth.

    Reicheld and Satmetrix have researched companies from dozens of industries. As part of its study, it matched consumers' survey responses about their likelihood to recommend the given companies' products and services to actual growth numbers from these companies. The results showed that, across industries, companies with more promoters (i.e., customers who are highly likely to recommend and advocate the products and services) than detractors (i.e., customers who are less likely to recommend or advocate the products and services) grew more rapidly than their competitors. www.netpromoter.com/site/np/ ultimate.jsp (accessed December 14, 2008), www.netpromoter.com/ site/np/metric.jsp (accessed December 14, 2008).

11

Building a Social Media Campaign

For many organizations, establishing a presence in social media is akin to learning a foreign language and assimilating to a new culture. Communicating with networking agents requires an understanding of social media's language codes, social dynamics, and acceptable behavior. As in any acculturation process, connecting with target audiences through social media takes time and effort. To be accepted by networking agents and to be recognized as a credible, trustworthy source, brand representatives need to find their own footing in social media and be present on dynamic platforms such as blogs, forums, and social networks.

Tip

To be accepted in social media, act like networking agents do. Publish and socialize online.

There are five fundamental components of building a social media campaign. After listening to consumer buzz online and determining the premise of your campaign, choose a platform to start sharing your messages. Stay tuned in to your audience's needs and attitudes. Keep updating your social media base with new content and offer value to your followers. Your audience will grow as you lead with actionable content, demonstrate your expertise, and make meaningful contributions to ongoing conversations.

The following are essential components of launching a social media campaign:

1. Set up shop and create a base. Start with a blog or social network page.
2. Understand what matters to people and acknowledge current events.
3. Update your content regularly.
4. Stick to your topic of expertise.
5. Inform networks and lead them to take action.

Set Up Shop and Create a Base in Social Media

When designing a social media campaign, consider the types of information you can offer to networking agents. Start by creating a base in social media—a blog, a social network profile, or a dynamic Web site—that introduces your brand, conveys your key messages, and shows that you are accessible and open to dialogue. Your online presence will underscore your commitment to the brand you are promoting and the cause you are looking to advance. Your blog, social network profile, or Web page will give networking agents the chance to get to know your brand, conduct their research, reference your information in their online and offline conversations, and revisit your Web site areas with questions and comments.

When communicating with networking agents, you can have one-to-one conversations with them through e-mail or phone. Your social media areas will also enable you to update information with ease and disseminate news fast. When reading and commenting on networking agents' posts, your social media area will indicate that you are part of the same ecosystem as the networking agents. Your commitment will set you apart from those who try to paste their messages on networking agents' online properties without any factual basis.

Tip

Whether posting a comment or a blog entry, add value to the conversation. Share new insights. Present your perspective. Do not copy and paste overt marketing messages to networking agents' areas.

Using a Blogger, TypePad, or WordPress template to start a blog, customizing the blog's interface, or building a Facebook fan page can be the first step of a social media campaign. The subsequent steps in building online presence come with the challenge of updating your content and corresponding with brand fans on a continuous basis.

Those looking for tips on how to fill up their online pages can take their cues from networking agents who command sizable audiences and make waves on the Internet and beyond. These cybercitizens talk and post about timely issues that concern large groups of people. They create impact by breaking news and organizing crowds to take action.

Understand What Matters to People and Acknowledge Current Events

The most visible networking agents communicate in an easily understandable fashion. They write about issues with which their readers can empathize. These agents touch a nerve, underscore widespread concerns, and tap into the news, both local and national. For instance, following the devastation of Hurricane Katrina, New Orleans Metro bloggers[1] reported from the affected areas and beyond, providing local and up-to-date accounts of the rescue efforts. Those looking for missing relatives filled the blogs' comments sections with names and reached deep into the blog reader networks to get information on their loved ones.

Sympathetic citizens beyond the New Orleans area also used blogs to communicate with those who wanted to help and organize efforts. Grace Davis from Santa Cruz, California, set up the Katrina blog[2] in August 2005 and kept it going for a year, coordinating volunteer efforts and directing care packages to the right shelters. If Ms. Davis had started a blog about her everyday life and used it to stay in touch with friends and family, she would have had a very limited audience. Using the same tools and focusing her efforts on emergency response, she attracted the attention of thousands and helped many more.

Whether blogging to promote a corporate or nonprofit brand, blog authors need to follow unfolding events closely and frequently comment on other blogs related to their fields. Taking the audience's pulse, calling out issues, and responding to other posts are ways bloggers start and sustain online conversations. Writer teams that support leading blogs, such as Techcrunch, Gizmodo, Boing Boing, Daily Kos, and TreeHugger, update entries at least several times a day, link to sources they highlight in their writing, post entries that comment on readers' reactions, and elaborate on corporate initiatives and social events. In doing so, they remain connected to an ever-widening circle of networking agents.

Tip

Stay abreast of news. Write about how current events might affect people and business.

Update Your Content Regularly

To maintain a connection with the audience, a common rule of thumb for those blogging to build their social media presence is to post a new entry at least once a week. Charlie, a New York–based entrepreneur, is an example of a successful networking agent who follows this rule. Enthused by all things digital, he lives and breathes the Internet. His blog, This Is Going to Be Big, consists of daily commentary on the latest and greatest developments in digital communications.

Charlie features new widgets and software applications on his blog and shares a great deal of his personal taste for music, books, and other media through listings on his blog. He links to his favorite blogs. His collection of readers' photos serves as a road map to people who matter in his personal and professional space.

He updates his blog almost every day and encourages his readers to sign up for his news. He draws his offline contacts to his online space.

Charlie touts the number of his subscribers—nearly 3,000[3]—near the title of his blog. Even if he does not have time to draft a full entry, he blasts a brief list of links to articles he has read and found compelling. He connects with his virtual audience on a regular basis without missing a beat.

Another New Yorker who is tenacious about updating his blog posts is Zach Brooks of Midtown Lunch. Any food lover who has lived or worked in Manhattan's midtown knows its limited and pricey lunch choices. Savory and filling dishes under $10 are hard to find in the area.

Zach helps thousands of employees and residents uncover new menu items as he scans the streets between Korea Town and Central Park, spanning from 3rd to 8th Avenues. He posts several entries on affordable and tasty finds every workday. He gives updates to his readers about their favorite locations.

Food talk drives many to Zach's blog. His readers are not too shy to comment on his entries and give him their two cents about his recommendations. In February 2009 alone, more than 140,000 people visited Midtown Lunch.[4]

Tip

Do not worry about posting lengthy pieces to your blog. Being in touch with your audience on a regular basis is more important. Try to write a new entry at least once a week.

Stick to Your Topic of Expertise

Continuing discussions on a single theme, such as motherhood challenges, economic development, or promoting a green lifestyle, establishes expertise and increases visibility in major search engines' listings. As relevant commentary accumulates in a blog space and other online sources link to it, the blog goes up the search engine ranks. For instance, Heather Armstrong, a stay-at-home mom in Utah, maintains her position as a top-100 blogger in the blog search engine Technorati's rankings with her blog Dooce.[5] Heather's sharp sense of humor and diligent chronicling of her family life and personal challenges resonate with many who follow her blog. Heather lost her job because she blogged about her coworkers. Today, the blog's advertising revenue supports her family.

When writer Amy Tenderich was diagnosed with Type 1 diabetes in 2003, she promised herself that she would enjoy life more. She charged on and started sharing the information she had been gathering about the disease through her blog Diabetes Mine.[6] She aptly called her blog a "gold mine of straight talk and encouragement for people living with diabetes." As she repeatedly posted about the challenges of living with diabetes and offered useful information for people with diabetes, Amy's blog drew a vast number of patients, caregivers, and other diabetes bloggers. Today, Diabetes Mine ranks among the leading health blogs[7] and has been featured in national media outlets such as the *Wall Street Journal*, the *New York Times*, and Fox News.

Tip

Do not try to be all things to all people. Write about what you know best. Speak to a targeted audience.

Inform Networks and Lead Them to Action

Marketers often debate whether content or distribution is the leading element in appealing to an audience. When it comes to spreading word of mouth online, there are three components that are intertwined and equally important: content, community, and communication. The message content has to inform the community and lead them to click, donate, purchase, download, or join a club, among other types of activities.

Members of the women's blogging network BlogHer[8] carry a wide variety of online conversations on the community Web site and on their individual blogs. They write about their family lives, companies, and social issues such as gender politics, health care, careers, and finance, among other topics. They review the products and services listed under the special offers section of the Web site. Yet the power of these outspoken women becomes most evident when they are organized around a cause.

When the online directory Find.com[9] wanted to raise funds for Doctors Without Borders, it turned to the BlogHer community and asked members to search for an item using its search engine. The company matched each search with a dollar donation to Doctors Without Borders. BlogHers rushed to the organization's help. While using Find.com, the women bloggers encouraged their peers to enlist others and help through their blogs. As a result, the BlogHers raised more than $10,000 and helped Doctors Without Borders buy and distribute more than 10,000 malaria vaccines in designated areas across developing countries.

Today, the BlogHer community includes 2,500 bloggers and attracts millions of readers through content partnerships.[10] Organizations may not always have the means to have the force of such a vast online network behind them. Yet, with the help of social media tools, the power of one creative mind may be enough to turn a business around.

Tip

Ask your readers to join you on a mission. Offer them ways to create change with a few clicks.

When her worm-composting business was losing money, Heather Gorringe of Lower Blakemere Farm in Herefordshire chose not to listen to her accountant, who thought she should close shop. She believed in her small company and her marketing ideas. She lived in a village of 63 people, but she thought she could reach more people through the Web and increase the number of leads for the business.

She and her partner fired the accountant and went on to use their Web site to reach green customers around the globe. Heather started a blog, but being more of a talker than a writer, she soon discovered the ease of reaching new audiences through podcasts. She started producing these audio chats from her couch at her farmhouse, using her personal computer. Her husband, Phil the Farmer, made regular appearances on her podcast shows, adding to the entertainment and giving listeners a fuller picture of country living in England.[11]

Heather's business—Wiggly Wigglers[12]—continues to thrive while she keeps talking with Web users who want to learn about farming, building better gardens, and preserving the planet. Wiggly Wigglers' group page on the social networking site Facebook has more than 1,300 active members[13] who communicate directly with a Wiggly Wigglers discussion moderator and receive updates from Heather in their in-boxes. Heather and Wiggly Wigglers' online presence foster the company's brand across geographies and complement the sales that come through catalog orders.

Tip

Be sure to expand your online portfolio to include multiple dialogue channels. Reach a variety of networks by blogging, tweeting, podcasting, and sending messages to your fans on social networking Web sites.

As these examples show, building a social media campaign goes beyond creating a one-time spark. It is unlike blasting a message to a long list of e-mails. Establishing a social media identity is similar to joining a new club, starting friendships, and growing the number and quality of those relationships over time. Sharing information, offering valuable experiences, and engaging in conversation help build brands in social media. It takes continuous effort to post fresh content and seek new online connections. Social media efforts merit an authentic, credible voice that can turn networking agents into believers, supporters, and recruiters.

Notes

1. Metro Blogging, http://neworleans.metblogs.com (accessed December 18, 2008).
2. Hurricane Disaster Direct Relief, http://gracedavis.typepad.com/katrinablog (accessed December 8, 2008).

3. This Is Going to Be BIG, www.thisisgoingtobebig.com (accessed December 18, 2008 and May 24, 2009).
4. Midtown Lunch, http://midtownlunch.com/about (accessed March 22, 2009).
5. Dooce, www.dooce.com (accessed March 19, 2009).
6. Diabetesmine, www.diabetesmine.com/about (accessed March 19, 2009).
7. eDrugSearch.com, www.edrugsearch.com/edsblog/healthcare100 (accessed March 19, 2009).
8. BlogHer, www.blogher.com (accessed December 18, 2008).
9. Find.com, www.find.com (accessed December 18, 2008).
10. BlogHer Ads, www.blogherads.com/for-advertisers (accessed March 19, 2009).
11. Heather's Wiggly Wigglers podcasts can be downloaded from iTunes.com.
12. Wiggly Wigglers, www.wigglywigglers.co.uk (accessed December 18, 2008).
13. Wiggly Wigglers' Facebook data was accessed March 16, 2009.

CHAPTER

12

Measuring Reach and Impact of Online Word of Mouth

During consumer-generated media's infancy, being present in this space put companies ahead of their competitors and singled out organizations for prospective donors and supporters. Many treated their social media initiatives as branding exercises without measuring return on their investments. Today's social media landscape is significantly more cluttered and complex than its early days. Social networks command millions of members. Leading blogs are published in multiple languages. Well-known newspapers and magazines are asking their editorial staff to write columns and blog entries.

The abundance of content that is easy to access and consume makes launching and sustaining noteworthy online projects challenging. As social media matures, the need to measure online word of mouth and demonstrate success becomes indisputable.

Measuring online word of mouth helps media planners recognize this field as a marketing channel that yields returns. When planners, brand managers, and C-suite executives see how online word of mouth programs reach significant numbers of people, create noticeable impact, and contribute to brands' longevity and sales, they can dedicate more resources to this domain.

Designing a Measurement Plan

A comprehensive measurement plan should consist of three parts—gauging the audiences' reactions to the brand before, during, and after the campaign. The first step in measuring online word of mouth is to listen and monitor audience chatter across blogs, forums, and social networks. This effort helps uncover existing issues, attitudes, and behaviors. It marks the starting point for a campaign. The second step requires tracking the campaign's progress and studying the interaction between message senders and receivers. During this phase, marketers can take note of attitudinal and behavioral changes among their target audience. The third step involves comparing final campaign results with benchmark scores to demonstrate the momentum and change the campaign generated.

Before the Campaign

During the first research phase, marketers should take the consumer pulse and establish a point of reference. What are people talking about? Are the comments positive or negative? What are the current attitudes and behaviors involving the brand? Benchmarking as such helps determine standards for success and lays out a plan to hit communication goals in time.

For instance, on learning about simmering product issues through online word of mouth analysis, a company can decide to add and change features that address customer needs and communicate the product enhancements to their customers. This exploratory research can also help brands uncover new audience groups that have embraced their products and services but

Tip

Before launching an online word of mouth campaign, research what consumers are saying about the brand or issue on blogs and forums. Set a benchmark.

do not fit their typical customer profile. The results can guide organizations as they grow their supporter base, determine their marketing strategy, and choose the types of metrics and measures they need to verify progress.

During the Campaign

When managing campaigns, communication professionals should keep an eye on how their messages are received by their audience and note their networking agents' reactions to their promotions and offers. They should make sure to speak with relevant, outspoken audience groups to extend their messages to ever-widening circles.

Weekly and monthly checks on the volume and content of online conversations can inform marketers about the course of their campaign. These reviews give marketers the chance to tweak their tactics and address any issues that may arise.

Measuring word of mouth that takes place during the campaign reveals the quality of conversations and shows how online audiences are engaging with an issue or a brand. For instance, a study of buzz activity during a word of mouth campaign for Sonicare Essence toothbrush revealed multiple cycles of conversations. The first group of consumers who tested the product took the word about Sonicare Essence to their friends, who then passed the information along to their friends, and so forth. Researchers measured the number of conversational partners each circle of consumers reached. Keeping an eye on the field activity allowed them to account for the ripple effect. As a result, they were able to quantify the intensity of word of mouth and the level of engagement with the Sonicare Essence brand.[1]

Tip

During a campaign, track changes in online word of mouth volume, messages, and relays.

After the Campaign

Tracking a campaign's success gives marketers the opportunity to compare results before and after they disseminate their messages. Following the campaign, they can review the latest Web activity reports, refer back to their benchmark measures, and conduct a survey to evaluate the changes in key metrics. It is important to look at the same core variables in a post-campaign study as in the first phase of the study, to do an accurate comparison and to tell the difference the campaign made.

The following sections of this chapter cover the fundamental methods, measures, and metrics marketers can use when looking for trends in networking agents' conversations. Exhibit 12.1 provides a blueprint for showing online word of mouth programs' success from inception to conclusion.

Exhibit 12.1 Elements of Online Word of Mouth Measurement

Design	Methods	Measures	Metrics
• Before	• Keyword searches	• Reach	• Volume of online posts
• During	• Online monitoring		• Number of unique visitors
• After	• Audience surveys		• Conversations
	• Web reports		• Relays
			• Number of bookmarks
		• Relevance	• Authority
			• Influence
			• Engagement
			• Topicality
			• Tone
		• Outcome	• Visibility
			• Awareness
			• Affinity
			• Customer satisfaction
			• Intention to act
			• Action

Tip

Be consistent when measuring pre- and post-campaign results. Stick to the same core metrics to compare results and show progress.

Methods

Methods are measurement approaches that help marketers find the answer to a research question. It is important to choose the appropriate method that will yield meaningful data. When measuring online word of mouth, organizations can run online searches, track conversations with deep-diving software, or turn to professional research companies to conduct audience surveys.

Desktop Key Word Searches

To get a top-level reading of online buzz about a brand or event, communication professionals can determine a set of key words their audiences are likely to use when commenting on a product, service, or issue. They can plug in these key words to blog search engines such as Technorati.com, Icerocket.com, and Google's Blogsearch[2] along with forum search engines such as BoardTracker.[3] They can read about online audiences' reactions by reviewing the results. They can learn who is talking about their topic. They can analyze the context in which networking agents are mentioning their brands.

At times, desktop key word search results may be too varied and scattered to evaluate and synthesize. They may not always

Tip

To get a preliminary read on buzz, plug in key words to Technorati.com.

provide researchers with deep information. Yet this rudimentary research approach can provide some fast answers to those facing tight budgets and timelines.

Online Monitoring Analyses

To conduct more in-depth analyses, marketers need to work with professional research firms that specialize in consumer-generated media analysis. These research firms use proprietary software to drill down on issues and collect vast amounts of online posts. They have intellectual and technical resources to sift through data and organize information in meaningful ways. Their reports allow marketers to gauge the volume of online conversation on key issues, learn the topics networking agents frequently discuss, and identify the most authoritative and influential networking agents who drive conversations. These research firms can also delve into competitive analyses, comparing brands' standing on various topics.

Partnering with a research firm that can track consumer-generated media is particularly helpful in gathering trended data and noticing simmering issues before they turn into crises. While practical online alert tools such as Google Alerts inform users every time a key word is used in a given article, investing in ongoing online monitoring studies can give organizations the advantage of noticing trends as they emerge, before they spread to mainstream outlets.

Analysts who conduct online conversation analyses review representative samples of online posts and code them for tone, polarity, and topics. Their monitoring reports include quotes from consumer posts that exemplify main trends and leave readers with a more colorful, textured understanding of key concepts. Another advantage of working with consumer-generated media research firms is to have access to industry experts. These professionals can provide insights about a given company or organization's standing in social media vis-à-vis its competitors. They can elaborate on how networking agents typically react to issues in various categories, based on their former research and observations.

Online monitoring analyses give marketers a comprehensive, scientific, and in-depth review of consumer conversations about their brands in social media. These findings can serve as benchmarks, track progress, set expectations for future communication campaigns, and support other marketing projects. Online word of mouth can even predict offline success. Nielsen Online's study of relationships between blog buzz, marketing support, and sales in the consumer packaged goods industry has found that incorporating buzz-related data into analyses improves sales forecasts' accuracy.[4]

Tip

Partner with a research firm to get in-depth, quantitative online buzz analyses.

Audience Surveys

A more traditional way of measuring online word of mouth is by surveying a representative sample of the target audience. The survey can be conducted online or offline. As in ongoing online monitoring analyses, researchers can field the survey on a regular basis and provide marketers with periodic updates. The survey can include questions about the audience's awareness of a brand or an issue, their attitudes toward certain products and services, their online habits, or their intentions to make recommendations and purchases.

Satmetrix, a research company that specializes in measuring customer loyalty, uses survey methodology to find connections between word of mouth, customer referrals, and sales. Satmetrix researchers uncover the percentage of consumers who make positive and negative recommendations about a product. They show how referrals affect consumer spending and sales.[5]

Web Activity Reports

When building online properties that will serve as a base camp for communicating with networking agents, marketers should also plan to have a system in place to get Web activity reports on a regular basis. Tools such as Google Analytics, Woopra, Compete, and Site Meter offer affordable ways to get detailed analyses on the number of Web site visitors and the most viewed Web pages.

The log reports offer clues about Web site engagement, showing the average amount of time users spend in a given Web area. Lists of Web sites that refer visitors to the base camp reveal audiences' online paths. Traffic reports can also point to new marketing strategies to draw additional audiences. Information on Web sites that refer the most number of visitors to the base camp can help marketers optimize their Web sites for search engines and identify profitable online partnerships.

Measures

A measure represents a collection of data points or observations. Organizations that gauge word of mouth effectively base their communications' impact on reach, relevance, and outcome measures. They track the number of people who receive and pass along their messages, quantify the percentage of their target audience among the population they reach, and match outcomes with initial goals to determine success.

Reach

Campaign reach encompasses the number of people who read, consume, and pass along messages they find online. Web site and blog visitor numbers can serve as campaign reach estimates. Yet a more comprehensive reach calculation should account for several generations of word of mouth—online and offline.

Tip

Account for multiple waves of word of mouth when calculating reach.

Relevance

Blogs and forums are micromessaging platforms. They rarely command the size of audience that traditional media channels obtain. They speak to niche and narrow segments. Yet they present the chance to reach specific interest groups who are highly engaged in conversation and hungry for information. Besides targeting online media outlets that garner large audiences, marketers should also consider reaching out to blogs and forums that pertain to their topic area and serve as gathering places for online enthusiasts and networking agents.

For instance, Café Mom—an online network that attracts 8 million unique visitors a month[6]—offers marketers the opportunity to connect with moms as these women discuss issues that matter the most to them, such as pregnancy, adoption, children's health, and working from home. Care2 is a 10-million-people network of socially conscientious Internet users who care about healthy and green living, as well as human and animal rights. Members of this community have gathered more than 34 million signatures for online petitions.[7] Communication professionals who can rally these dedicated online community members behind their causes can significantly boost their campaign results.

Tip

Focus campaigns on niche but highly relevant sites to get in touch with enthusiasts and networking agents.

Outcome

Before measuring an online word of mouth program, marketers should consider the type of outcome that will define success for them. A noteworthy increase in sales is the desired outcome of most marketing initiatives. Yet audiences take numerous steps between learning about a product and making a purchase. Consider these attitudinal and behavioral steps as part of the campaign outcome that would add richness to results and provide marketers with a comprehensive picture of their success. For instance, increase in awareness of an issue, change from a negative to a favorable attitude toward a brand,

Tip

Sales do not have to be the only outcome of an online word of mouth campaign. Gauge changes in buzz levels, sentiments, and intentions to recommend.

intention and willingness to try a product or recommending a company can underscore significant accomplishments.

Metrics

Metrics are measurement units. They are the data points and observations that make up measures. Every online word of mouth measure encompasses a series of metrics. Marketers can employ the following metrics to evaluate what they create and change.

Reach Metrics

The most frequently used metrics in measuring online word of mouth campaigns' reach are numbers of blog posts, comments, Web site visits, online community memberships, downloads, peer-to-peer referrals, and additions to social bookmarking sites such as Digg and Delicious. The following are five basic questions marketers can ask to collect the right pieces of information and determine reach:

1. *Volume.* How many posts are there?
2. *Audience size.* How many people read these posts?
3. *Conversations.* How many conversations take place that mention the brand, the message, or the issue?
4. *Word of mouth relays.* How many people pass along information from these posts to their friends and family?
5. *Online trails.* How many people bookmark brand-related Web pages and posts?

Volume of Online Posts The numbers of unique Web site, blog, and forum posts that reference the brand, product, service, or issue indicate online word of mouth reach. Blog search engines and research firms' proprietary software tools count the number of posts. They show heat maps of where buzz accumulates and identify each source contributing to online buzz.

Tip

Use Nielsen Buzzmetrics' BlogPulse[8] to chart online buzz over the past year.

Number of Unique Visitors The number of unique Internet users who visit a corporate microsite, a portal, a blog, or a forum offers a proxy for the number of people an online communication campaign reaches. While it is not certain that everyone who visits the Web site has read the campaign messages or decided to take action, this number represents the widest population the campaign can reach through a given Web location.

Typically, established Web sites report the number of unique visitors they get per month and post these numbers on their properties for advertisers. If a Web site does not share this information publicly, then researchers can use free Web traffic tools such as Alexa, Quantcast, or Compete. These services provide top-level audience metrics on Web sites that are registered in their systems. There may be variances in their reports based on data collection methods and assumptions. For detailed and more customized information on Web site visitors, marketers can subscribe to reports from companies that specialize in online traffic analysis, such as HitWise, Nielsen NetRatings, and comScore.

Tip

Use Compete.com to compare multiple Web sites' traffic levels.

Conversations Online conversations stem from blog, social network, and message board posts and spread into comment areas. There are also many online conversations that take place in private forums and spill offline. Networking agents and their peers continue to carry the word as they chat face-to-face, speak on the phone, and send e-mails and instant and text messages.

Consumer-generated media search engines and research firms can trace online posts and comments. However, to gauge the full range of conversations a campaign generates, organizations need to conduct surveys and ask their audiences about the conversations they have online and offline. Through this method, they can drill down on the number of times consumers mention brands in their conversations. They can ask their audience where they held their conversations and what channels they used when disseminating information. They can uncover how networking agents spread news and cascade messages.

Tip

Conduct an audience survey to uncover consumers' online and offline conversations.

Relays and Word of Mouth Generations Online word of mouth can begin with a simple click that forwards an article or a review. According to the Word of Mouth Marketing Association's terminology framework, these pieces of marketing-relevant information consumers share are WOM units (word of mouth units).[9] Each time Internet users relay[10] a WOM unit to their peers, a new word of mouth generation begins and the WOM unit travels further. For instance, when a networking agent learns about a new product from an online community moderator and e-mails about the product to ten friends, he creates the first generation of word of mouth. When five of those ten friends each pass along the information to three of their friends, they propel the second generation of word of mouth (see Exhibit 12.2).

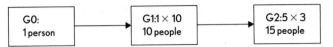

Exhibit 12.2 Word of Mouth Generations and Relays

When measuring reach, marketers can count the number of people who passed along their message and the number of word of mouth generations their messages lived. Each relay can signify additional value. Word of mouth generations reveal the process through which organizations gain supporters and acquire and retain customers.[11]

Tip

Conversations that extend for several generations of word of mouth bring incremental business value.

Online Bookmarks Networking agents use bookmarking Web sites to keep a running list of their favorite Web sites, online articles, and posts. They can keep these listings private or share their selections with the larger Internet universe. Social bookmarking Web sites, such as Digg, Delicious, Reddit, and Newsvine, are in fact dynamic consumer-generated news Web sites that show what Internet users consider noteworthy. When social bookmarking Web site users list a Web address, they bring that Web page to other users' attention. If the lister is a networking agent who is highly regarded by the community, other users add the Web page to their bookmarks and share it with their peers. The more users add a Web article to their accounts, the further the messages in that article spreads.

For instance, on April 5, 2009, a news article about the Airbus factory in Toulouse, France, made it to the top of the news listings

on Digg.com. The story that informed readers about the opening of the factory's assembly line to visitors originated from
the Australian Associated Press. It was picked up by the *Daily
Telegraph* and Australian News.com Web sites on April 3, 2009.[12]
Using the sharing tools News.com.au offers to readers, an avia-
tion enthusiast posted the link to the article on Digg. About 300
other Digg users followed this user and added the link to their
Digg accounts, making the article one of the most popular stories on the Web site within a couple of days. The Airbus factory
story spread from France and Australia to the worldwide Web,
thanks to social bookmarking.

Tip

Note listings and rankings on bookmarking sites to show how your news spreads.

Relevance Metrics

While it is a must to get a read on the number of people a communication campaign reaches online and to capture the amount
of activity it generates in social media, it is also crucial to understand that online conversations vary in terms of quality, credibility, depth, and tone. The authority and influence of online
conversationalists (e.g., networking agents) can have an impact
on the way an online story spreads and engages audience groups.
The following is a list of relevance metrics that can help marketers
steer their messages toward groups that matter:

- *Authority.* Do your targets have a broad base of followers
  who quote and link back to them?
- *Influence.* Do consumers follow your targets' advice?
- *Engagement.* How do Web site visitors interact with the
  target content?

- *Topicality.* Does the target publish content tied to your concept, brand, or issue?
- *Tone.* Does the online post carry a positive, negative, or neutral tone?

Authority The number of Web sites, blogs, and posts that link and point to a blog confirms its authority. When writers quote and reference a source, they deem that information outlet reliable and useful. Similarly, every link that points to a social media address boosts that source's authority. The links indicate that readers trust what they read and want to share the information with their networks. Brands that launch blogs and release news online can earn networking agents' approval as Internet users list them among their favorites and well-known blogs cite them.

When measuring results, it is possible to check the number of links pointing to a given Web address by using popular search engines and counting manually. Yet a more precise and consistent method to measure blog authority would be to enter the blog's address to the Technorati search engine and note the authority score the search engine calculates for that blog. Desktop monitoring tools such as Radian6 and BuzzLogic also measure the number of in-bound links to blogs from brand Web sites, news Web sites, forums, and other blogs.

High authority scores signify broad online networks and wide reach. A common question for researchers is what constitutes a benchmark for a high authority score. This may vary depending on topic and industry area. When planning to reach out to blogs, marketers should research the span of

Tip

Use Technorati.com's authority scores to show the number of links pointing to a blog.

authority scores for blogs that cover their topic area and target those that have higher than average scores. For instance, if blogs that cover topics related to the New York City real estate market have scores ranging from zero to 600, then marketers looking to promote real estate services in this area can focus on blogs with scores 300 and higher.

Influence An online source's influence is tied to its popularity, authority, credibility, and trustworthiness. An influential source can change its readers and followers' perceptions and convince them to take action. Influential sources' recommendations turn into positive views and purchases. Their warnings spread fast and can prevent people from choosing a brand. Influencers can change their votes on a given issue.

Many automated consumer-generated media monitoring systems calculate influence based on complex algorithms that factor in a mix of reach and relevance metrics. If marketers do not have the luxury of relying on an automated system that can rank social media sources in order of influence, they can create their own evaluation criteria. For instance, they can check the blog's authority score on Technorati, study the author's background, and review the blogger's presence on social networks. Following suit, they can choose to engage bloggers who are linked, authoritative, knowledgeable, and popular.

Tip

Create your own formula for online influence by checking bloggers' authority scores, professional backgrounds, and reach.

Engagement Internet users' interactions with online content and other Web site visitors indicate their level of engagement. There are popular ways of quantifying engagement, such as measuring the amount of time spent on a Web site and counting the number of comments online posts garner. Yet marketers can gain more in-depth knowledge about their online audiences by going beyond basic Web metrics. Online media engagement can be a qualitative measure that gives directional information about consumers' online experience as well as a quantitative measure that predicts purchasing behavior.

To understand the nature of users' interaction with the blog content, marketers can study comments' tone and length. They may find a detailed, positive review more meaningful than a neutral or negative monosyllabic comment. Furthermore, they can classify the topics commentators discuss and analyze the quality of information these social media agents share. What are their main topics of discussion? Do they touch on key issues? Do they repeat marketing-related messages? Are they in agreement with the post? Do they link to other sources? Comments that repeat, relay, and enhance key messages would suggest that online audiences are highly engaged.

Compelling online content can draw comments from a wide variety of Internet users. Yet not every reader will choose to comment. In the absence of a skillful moderator, a handful of outspoken individuals can dominate online discussions. Therefore, the number of comments on a blog or forum should not be used as a definitive score for reach and engagement. Reading and analyzing small samples of online commentary can give marketers directional insights about their audience's attitudes and potential behaviors.

Meanwhile, surveys that probe audiences' overall media consumption and word of mouth patterns can yield scientific, quantitative data on engagement. The Simmons' Multimedia Engagement Study provides proof. As part of this research, Simmons asked more than 12,000 respondents about 523 television programs and networks, 150 magazine titles, and 293 Web sites through phone and online surveys. The study also delved into the social interactions (i.e., word of mouth) and subsequent purchases the media channels spurred.

Simmons researchers identified four aspects of media channels that engaged audiences:

1. Being inspirational
2. Trustworthy
3. Life enhancing
4. Providing personal time out

They uncovered a relationship between these facets of engagement, word of mouth, and intention to purchase. For instance, the more audiences found media to be life enhancing, the more they talked about what they read and heard. As word of mouth increased, so did audiences' likelihood to purchase the products and services mentioned in the media. For the Internet channel, researchers found that engaging online content that enhanced audiences' lives and gave them personal time out drove word of mouth. These types of online engagements also led to purchases through word of mouth.[13]

Tip

Online audiences find life enhancing content highly engaging.

Topicality Marketers can analyze online posts and evaluate the degree to which the Web content contains their campaign's key messages. Those posts that reference campaign topics and include core messages would be more valuable than those posts that cite competitors, diverge from the topic, and do not relay marketers' messages.

Tone of Online Conversations/Posts Marketers can gain a perspective on how their audiences are receiving their messages by evaluating the tone of consumer-generated media.

Tip

On-topic posts are about key campaign messages.

They can develop and follow a classification system based on their communication goals. For instance, they can set up a paradigm where factual posts repeat marketing-related information as is, positive posts go beyond the information marketers disseminate and indicate consumers' enthusiasm with upbeat remarks, and negative posts include disapproving comments about the topic.

Successful social media campaigns aimed at promoting products and services should generate mostly positive and factual posts, indicating customer satisfaction and encouraging others to purchase. Campaigns involving public policy and social issues should show that online audiences agree with the campaign's perspectives and they intend to confirm their opinions with their votes.

Tip

Positive posts include key campaign messages and carry enthusiasm.

Outcome Metrics

When designing online word of mouth campaigns, marketers should connect their goals with measurable outcomes that will indicate they have successfully completed their campaigns. Determining the outcome variable that will gauge their achievement can help them choose the right measurement tools from the beginning and stay on course when interacting with their audiences. The following are tangible outcomes that point to changes online word of mouth campaigns can create:

- *Online visibility.* Did your Web site's search engine ranking improve?
- *Awareness.* Is your target audience more likely to know about your brand?
- *Affinity.* Do more people among your audience like and prefer the brand?
- *Customer satisfaction.* Are your customers satisfied? Are they more satisfied than 6 to 12 months ago?
- *Intention to take action.* Is your audience ready to click, vote, or purchase?
- *Actions.* Has your audience been visiting your online properties, clicking through, voting, or purchasing?

Online Visibility Having a blog, being active on Twitter, or allowing customers to post reviews on a Web site broadens an organization's reach and increases its visibility online. Every addition to an online area—a press release, an article, a comment, or a post—provides search engines with new material to index and archive. Using search engine optimization tactics (e.g., buying advertisements on search engines, tagging, and writing Web content that includes words audiences frequently use to search) brings branded Web areas to users' attention. Word of mouth campaigns that facilitate online conversations and empower networking agents to contribute authentic content to these dialogues push relevant content up search engine ranks and increase organizations' online visibility.

Tip

Expanding your digital footprint improves search engine rankings.

Awareness When the goal is to introduce a new offering or to reach new groups and geographic areas, an increase in public awareness can be a campaign outcome. This basic metric confirms that information has disseminated and campaign messages have reached the target audience. Marketers can take awareness measures a step further and explore if there are any relationships between public awareness and brand likeability, intention to purchase, and actions people take after being exposed to information. They can look for connections between awareness and conversations, referrals, votes, purchases, and petition signatures.

Tip

Study the relationships between awareness, conversations, and referrals.

Affinity After increasing awareness of a brand, product, or issue, marketers can use online monitoring and survey methods to see if their audiences like the product, form a bond with the brand, and agree with their perspectives. For instance, an emerging brand that does not yet have much traction among networking agents can set goals to keep its customers highly satisfied and improve its likeability and affinity scores over time.

Strong brand affinity and dedication to a cause suggest a longer relationship with the organization. Those individuals who demonstrate high levels of affinity also have a high likelihood to issue recommendations, make purchases, and cast favorable votes. A study on brand advocates by Yahoo! shows that those consumers who are passionate about brands are more likely to search and spread information online. These individuals are also more likely than nonadvocates to be satisfied with their purchases and remain loyal to the brands they favor.[14]

Tip

Track likeability over time and invite those who show strong affinity to become brand advocates.

Customer Satisfaction Online word of mouth is a reflection of relationships between brands and their audiences. It also reveals the interaction between networking agents and their peers. When outspoken online customers post about their experiences, they leave a trail of comments other shoppers can read before purchasing. Internet audiences, who have long-term, positive experiences with a brand, are bound to make recommendations about the brand's products and services. As satisfied customers, they will share their knowledge of what is best, most useful, and highest quality and turn their listeners into purchasers.

Companies can gain significant knowledge by tracking such online conversations and hearing what consumers have to say. They can also take their customers' pulse with surveys and ask them the degree to which they are satisfied with the organization, its products, and the services.

Tip

Ask customers what they are least satisfied with to start improving business and brand reputation.

Intention to Take Action According to social scientists Martin Fishbein and Icek Ajzen's Theory of Reasoned Action,[15] attitudes, norms, and intentions can indicate whether audiences will take action and follow a certain behavior. For instance, if people have a positive attitude toward volunteering and believe others would think well of them if they volunteered, then they would show strong intentions to volunteer.

Online word of mouth campaigns can be instrumental in changing audiences' intentions. Having information about special offers on a product can change consumers' attitudes and increase their intentions to purchase that particular brand. Being exposed to information about a political candidate can alter voters' perspectives, lead them to support the candidate, and increase their intentions to vote.

Positive changes in audiences' intentions to recommend, purchase, or support a social issue are real results. Communication professionals who want to predict their audiences' behavior can use surveys to measure consumers' attitudes, normative perceptions, and intentions to take action.

Tip

Measure audiences' intentions and remove barriers to action to give campaigns new direction.

Actions Online word of mouth campaigns yield recommendations, votes, and purchases. When organizations engage word of mouth agents and infuse networks with their messages, they hope to see an increase in sales and public support. To connect such outcomes with their marketing initiatives, communication professionals need to document their audiences' online behaviors and show online buzz can lead to posts, clicks, downloads, or offline actions such as votes, coupon redemptions, and in-store purchases. Marketers can review sales trends during and after the campaign and note any increases that correspond with online buzz volume. Political strategists can explore how visits to online information hubs affect votes, signatures, and donations.

Tip

To capture audiences' actions, follow their conversation trails online and offline. Survey them about their communications and latest brand-related activities.

The fundamental principle of measuring online word of mouth is to understand how and where audiences receive, harness, and pass along information. Exhibit 12.3 presents an overview of practical methods marketers can employ to capture online word of mouth campaign results.

Exhibit 12.3 Measuring Online Word of Mouth Campaign Results

Before the Campaign
- Monitor online buzz
- Conduct a benchmark survey among customers
- Identify your networking agents
- Measure the brand's Net Promoter Score with a survey tool

During the Campaign
- Continue to monitor online buzz
- Review brand/campaign Web site traffic and activities
- Take customers' pulse with periodic surveys
- Track peer-to-peer sharing activities online
- Follow up on networking agent communications and posts

After the Campaign
- Note change in search engine rankings
- Review and compare volume, tone, and quality of online buzz to pre-campaign measures
- Conduct a customer survey to measure impact on audience
- Review Web site activities
- Note recommendations and reviews networking agents post online and indicate in customer surveys
- Measure post-campaign Net Promoter Score through customer survey
- Track coupon redemptions (if applicable)
- Compare pre- and post-campaign sales figures (if applicable)

Notes

1. McGillin, Carl, and Oles, "Measuring the Ripple: Creating G2X Relay Rate and an Industry Standard Methodology to Measure the Spread of Word of Mouth Conversations and Marketing Relevant Outcomes," *Measuring Word of Mouth*; Word of Mouth Marketing Association, Vol. 3, 2007, pp. 37–45.
2. Google Blog Search, http://www.google.com/blogsearch (accessed December 21, 2008).
3. Board Tracker, http://www.boardtracker.com (accessed December 21, 2008).
4. Neiderhoffer, Kate, "The Origin and Impact of CPG New Product Buzz: Emerging Trends and Implications," *Measuring Word of Mouth*, Word of Mouth Marketing Association, Volume 3, 2007, pp. 106–112.
5. Satmetrix, "Net Promoter Economics: The Impact of Word of Mouth: Exploring the Relationship between Net Promoter and Word of Mouth in the Computer Hardware Industry," *Measuring Word of Mouth*, Word of Mouth Marketing Association, Volume 4, 2008, pp. 153–168.
6. Café Mom, http://www.cafemom.com/about/index.php (accessed March 29, 2009).
7. Care2.com, http://www.care2.com (accessed March 29, 2009).
8. BlogPulse, http://www.blogpulse.com (accessed April 12, 2009).
9. Word of Mouth Marketing Association; *Measuring Word of Mouth: Current Thinking on Research and Measurement of Word of Mouth Marketing*; Carl and Walter eds., Volume 4, 2008, p. 9.
10. Ibid.
11. Carl, Libai, and Ding, "Measuring The Value of Word of Mouth," *Measuring Word of Mouth*; Word of Mouth Marketing Association, Volume 4, 2008, pp. 65–75.
12. Plater, Diane, "The Ultimate Airplane Tour," *The Daily Telegraph*, April 3, 2009.
13. Kilger, Max, and A. Jolayne Sikes, "The Impact of Word of Mouth on Product Purchase Intent: The Relationships Among Word of Mouth, Media Engagement, and Product Purchase Intent," *Measuring Word of Mouth*, Word of Mouth Marketing Association, Volume 3, 2007, pp. 113–122.
14. Meeker, Heather, "Brand Advocates: An In-Depth Look at a Marketer's Valuable Online Influencer," *Measuring Word of Mouth*, Word of Mouth Marketing Association, Volume 3, 2007, pp. 124–130.
15. Ajzen, Icek, and Martin Fishbein, *Belief, Attitude, Intention, and Behavior: An Introduction to Theory and Research.* Reading, MA: Addison-Wesley; 1975.

Epilogue

THE FUTURE

In the past three decades, the Internet has grown from a niche tool to a widespread network used by more than one billion people worldwide (according to comScore, January 2009). What will the digital landscape look like in the future? Who will become networking agents? How will online influence affect companies' internal and external affairs? To what degree will online influence shape political and social agendas?

As more audiences gravitate to the Web to uncover new information and improve their lives, the value of online real estate will increase. Media companies are shifting from traditional to online outlets at an enormous speed. Dedicated blog editors and authors are building teams, turning their amateur space into professionally crafted online publications. Blog networks are becoming online publishing, opinion polling, and activism powerhouses. Institutional Web sites are adding discussion and community areas to support online customer services.

The Internet has transformed the flow of communications, turning computers into networking tools. Virtual messages cut across geographies and time zones in a matter of seconds, connecting disparate groups. Online conversations seep offline, contributing to knowledge hubs, amplifying power, and building movements. The number of organizations that use the Web to gain competitive advantage is growing exponentially. Political campaigns that mobilize voters through Twitter messages, retailers that ask mommy bloggers to review products, nonprofits that turn to social networks to raise funds, and small businesses that send coupons from Web sites to mobile phones are using this medium effectively.

Participating in social media begins with a user name and a password. Yet being noticed in this space and creating seismic change requires an understanding of online communications and word-of-mouth marketing. Networking agents are gate-keepers to online communities. They continuously add to their information sources. They feed news to their peers. They generate threads of online conversations. Those who can act as networking agents and harness the Internet's power in connecting people with resources will be tomorrow's success stories.

Appendix

AN ASSESSMENT WORKSHEET

The following 30 questions will serve as a guide as you prepare to launch your online word of mouth marketing programs. Fill in the answers to define your goals, describe your audience, and identify the methods that would generate conversations about your organization and brand. Use this form to create a blueprint for your social media communications and draw your online word of mouth marketing plan.

Stating Your Mission

1. What are your goals in launching this online word of mouth program?

2. What are the challenges facing your organization and brand?

3. What would you like to accomplish through social media?

4. What will success look like to your organization and brand?

Conducting Your Research

5. What are your current online activities? How do your stakeholders respond to these initiatives? What do they say about your organization and/or brand online? What is the volume and tone of these conversations?

6. What are your competitors doing online? What do their stakeholders say about them in social media channels? What is the volume and tone of these conversations?

7. Who is your target audience? How do they behave online? Which social media channels do they use?

8. Is there any news that might change the way your audience perceives your organization? What are the messages the media are sending to your audience?

9. What are the most trusted sources of communication for your audience? How does word of mouth rank among them? How do social media channels rank among them?

10. What constitutes influence among your online audience? Is it the way they communicate online and offline? Are there any demographic traits that might suggest influence? What sort of background should they have to be public opinion leaders?

11. Who among your online influencers are driving conversations and generating online buzz about your organization and brand?

Preparing Your Message

12. What are the fundamental traits of your brand?

13. How would you like your target audience to describe your organization?

14. What are the messages your competitors are delivering to your audience?

15. What is the message you need to share with your target audience to reach your goals?

Delivering Your Message

16. Which social media channels and platforms will you use to approach your audience?

17. Are your organization's Web properties (i.e., brand Web site, social networking pages, blog, etc.) up to date? Do they have content that contains your current messaging?

18. Do you have a list of your online influencers whom you would like to engage in online conversations?

19. What are the resources you need to reach out to your online influencers and start communicating with them one-on-one?

Managing Online Relations

20. Who will deliver your messages to your online influencers? How frequently will they do so?

21. Are there channels (i.e., a "Contact Us" section on the Web site, an e-mail address, a hotline, etc.) for your audience to send you their comments and feedback?

22. How will you track the responses you might get to your outreach?

23. Who will respond to comments and feedback from your online influencers?

24. How quickly can your organization respond to online comments? Which online channels can you use to respond? Is there an internal process you have to follow?

25. What types of activities will you create and launch online to keep your audience's interest and to sustain a dialogue with them?

Measuring Impact

26. Do you have benchmarking information about the quantity and quality of online conversations about your organization and brand?

27. Do you have an online buzz monitoring system in place? How frequently are you monitoring online conversations about your organization and brand? Do you need to increase the frequency in which you take your online audience's pulse?

28. Do you have the tools to monitor activity and track traffic on your online properties?

29. Will you need to survey your online audience to get their opinions about a concept or measure their offline word of mouth activities?

30. Which metrics will you use to capture the changes in your audience's behaviors and attitudes before and after your initiatives?

Index